THIS NOTEBOOK
BELONGS TO:

_____

_____

ERNEST CREATIVE DESIGNS

Copyright © 2019.
All right reserved. No part of this book or this book as a whole may be used, reproduced, or transmitted in any form or means without written permission from publisher.

LETTERS

A B C D E F G H I J
K L M N O P Q R S T U V
W X Y Z

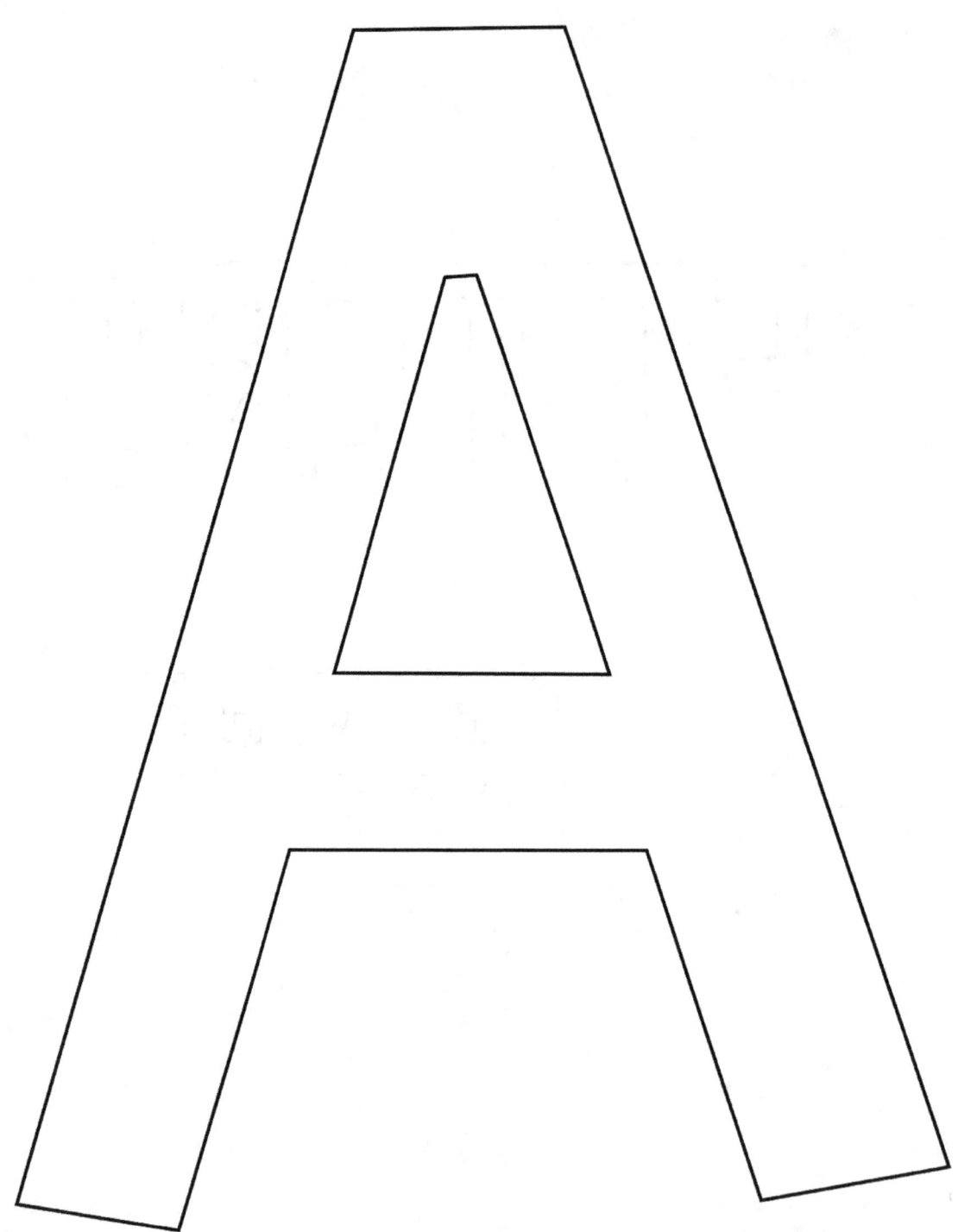

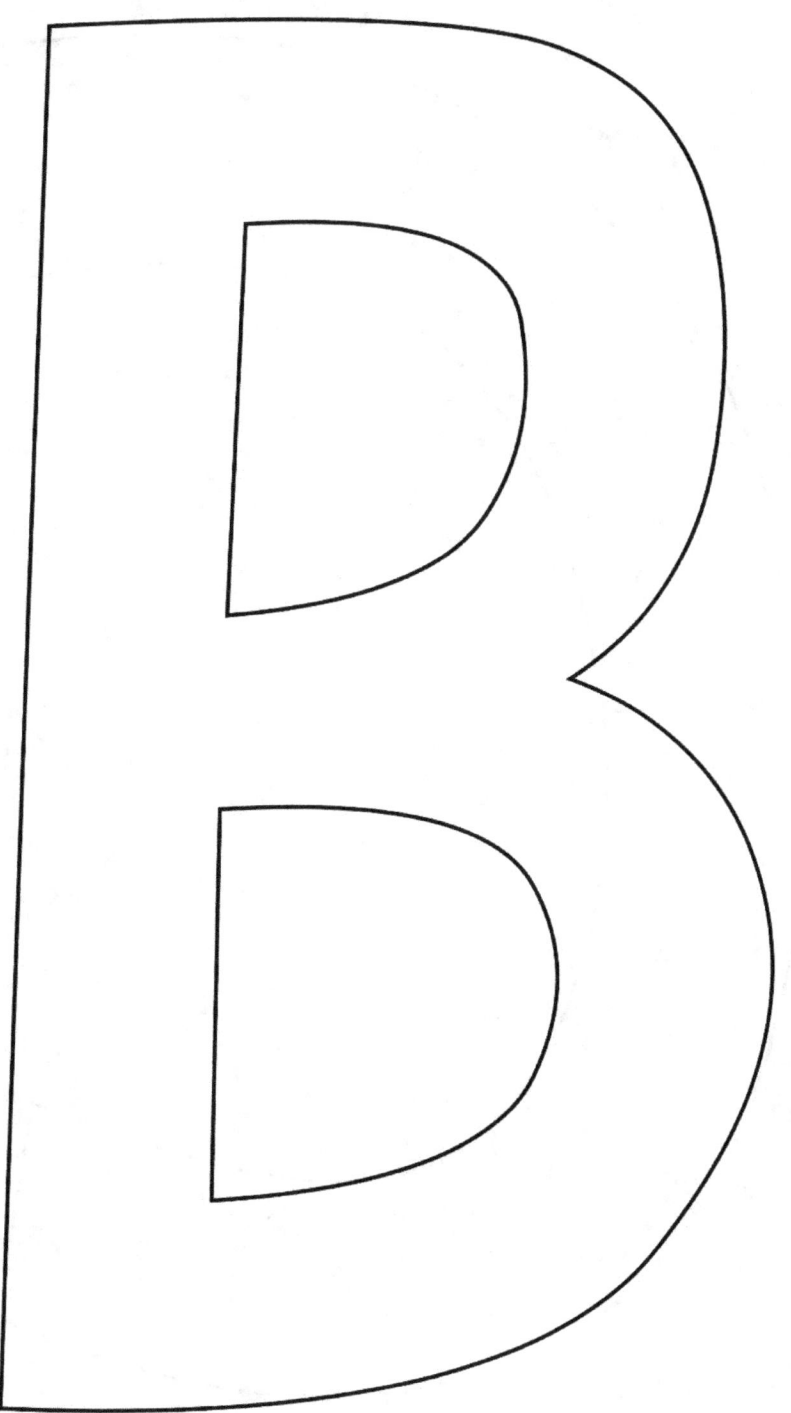

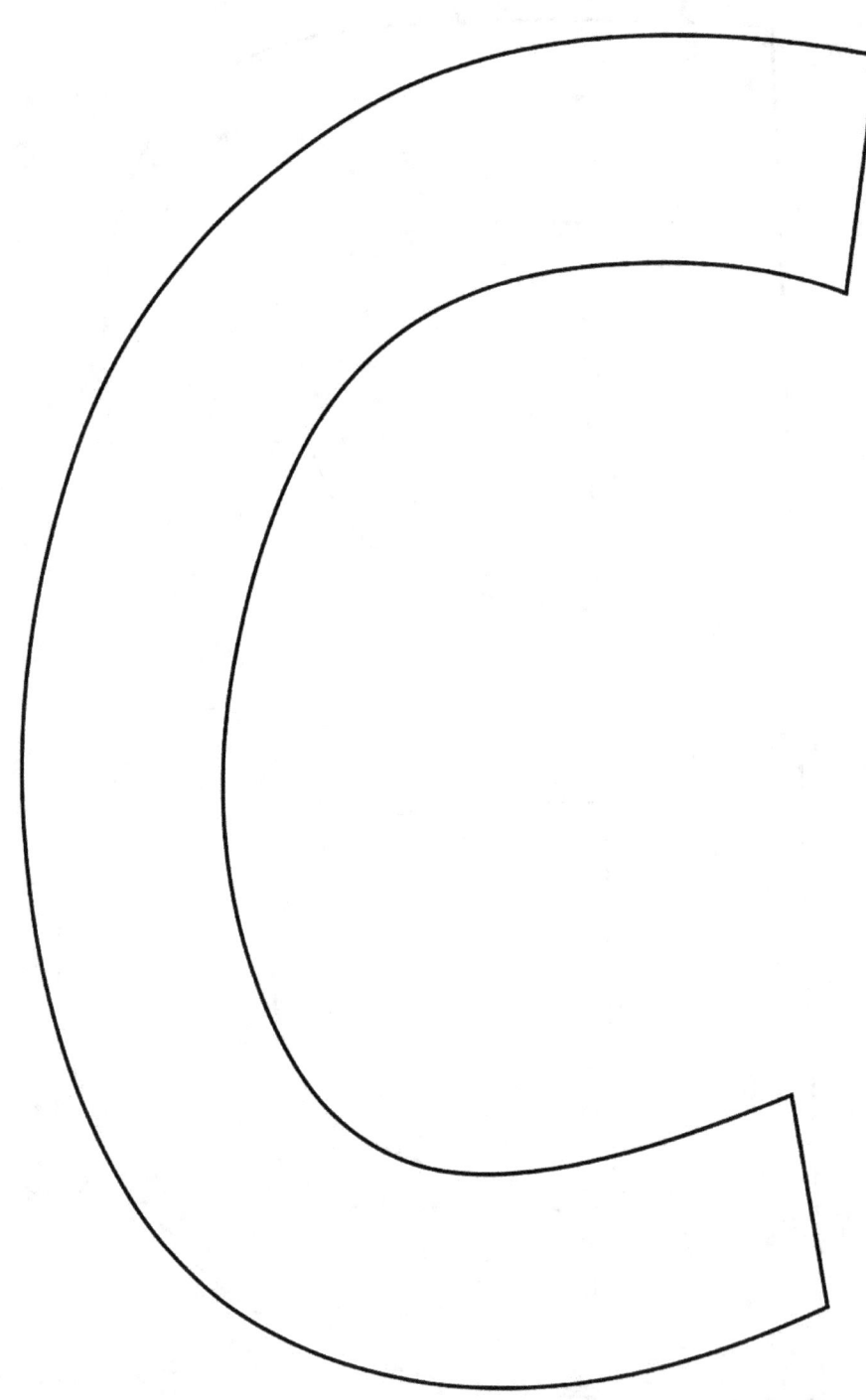

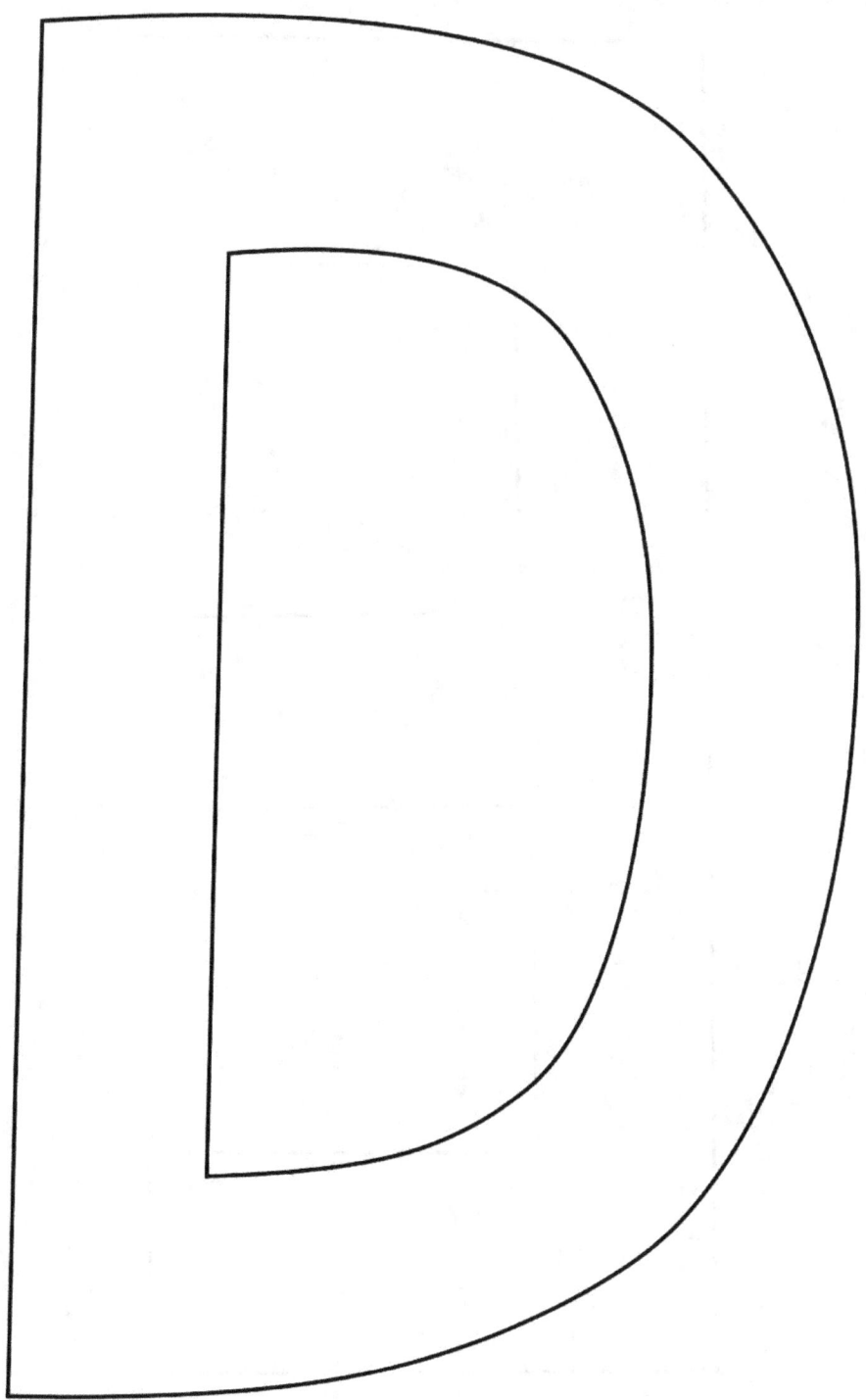

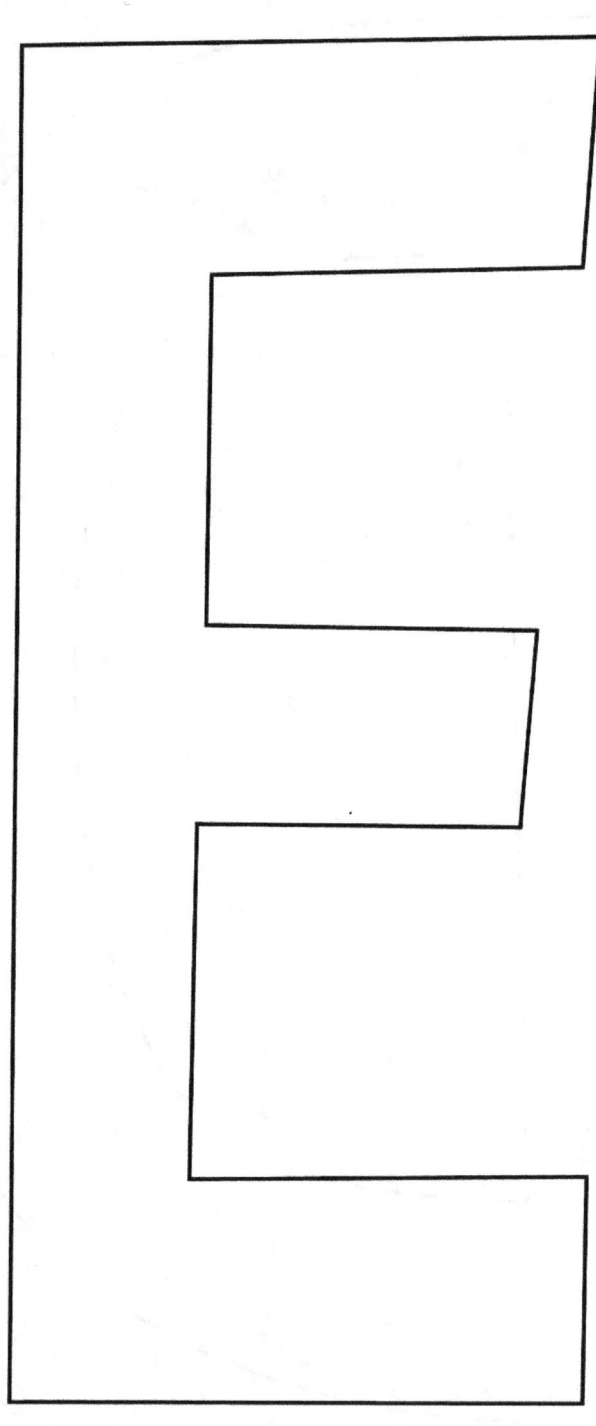

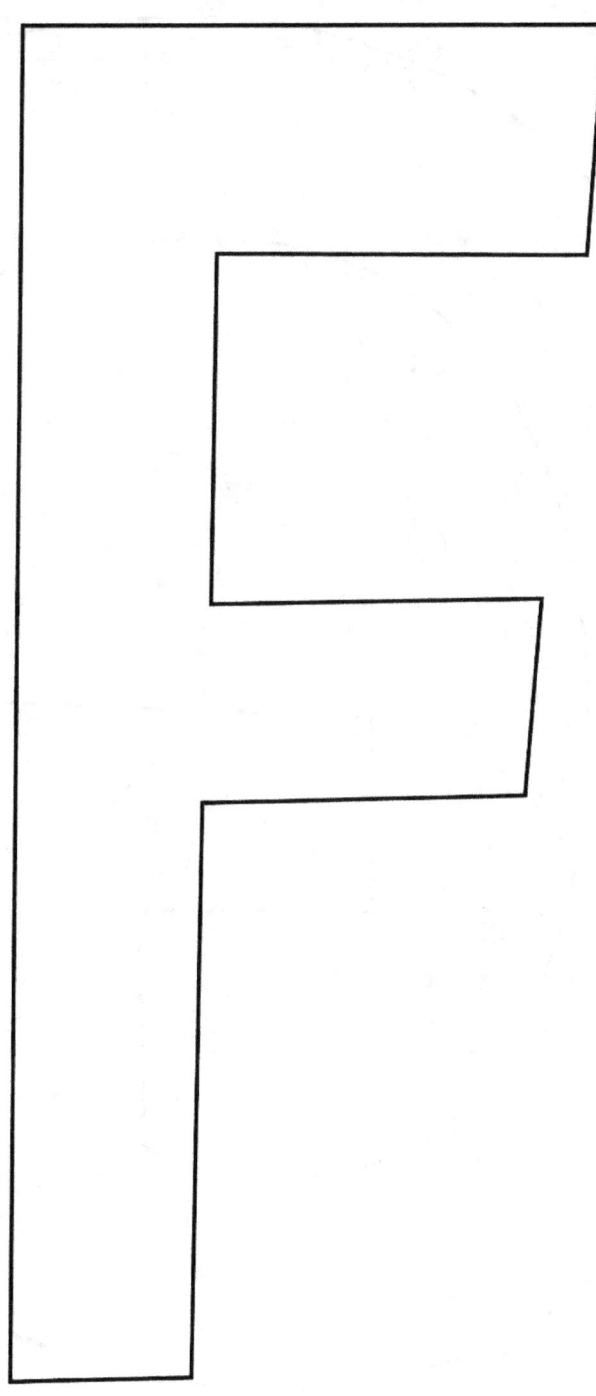

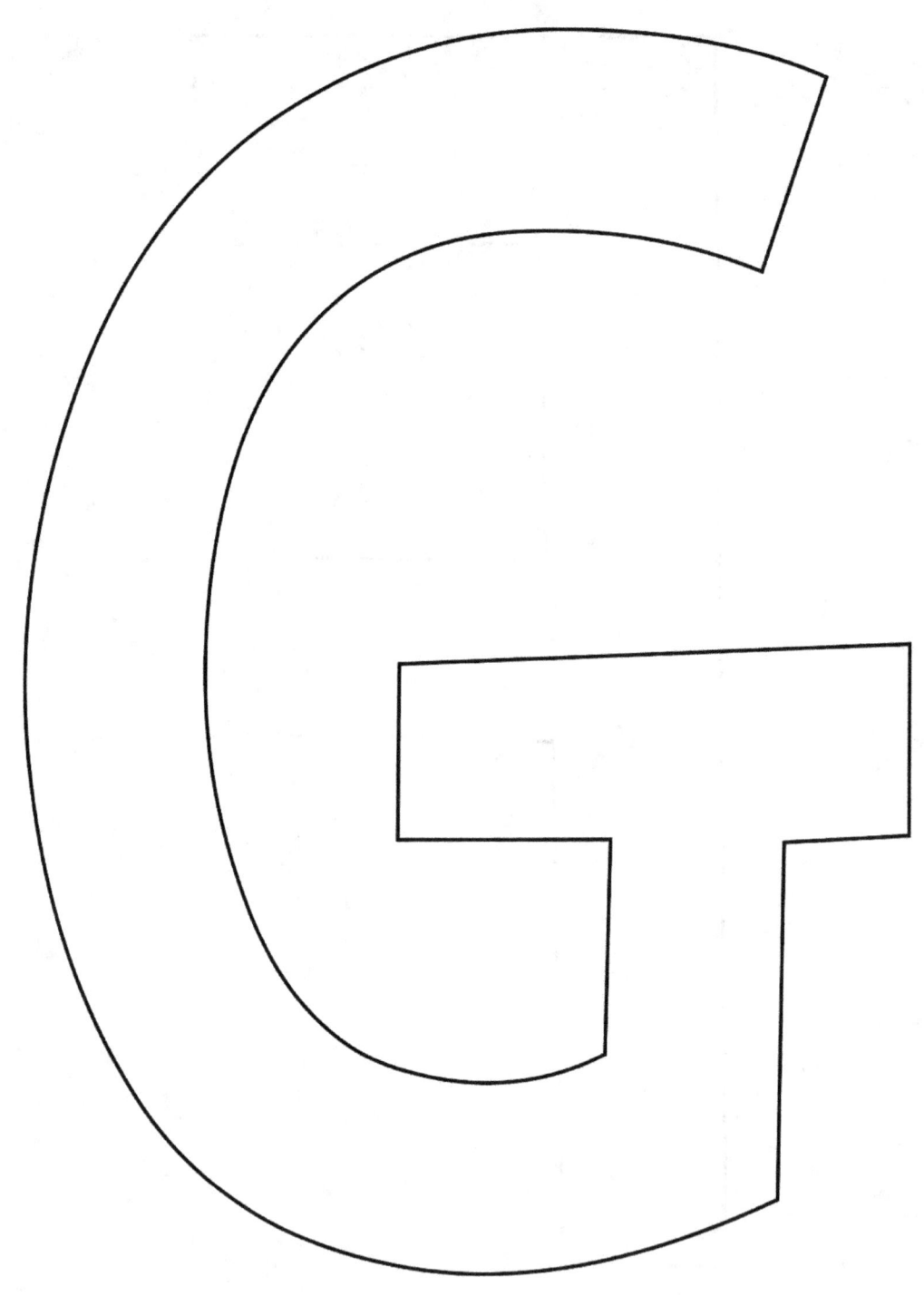

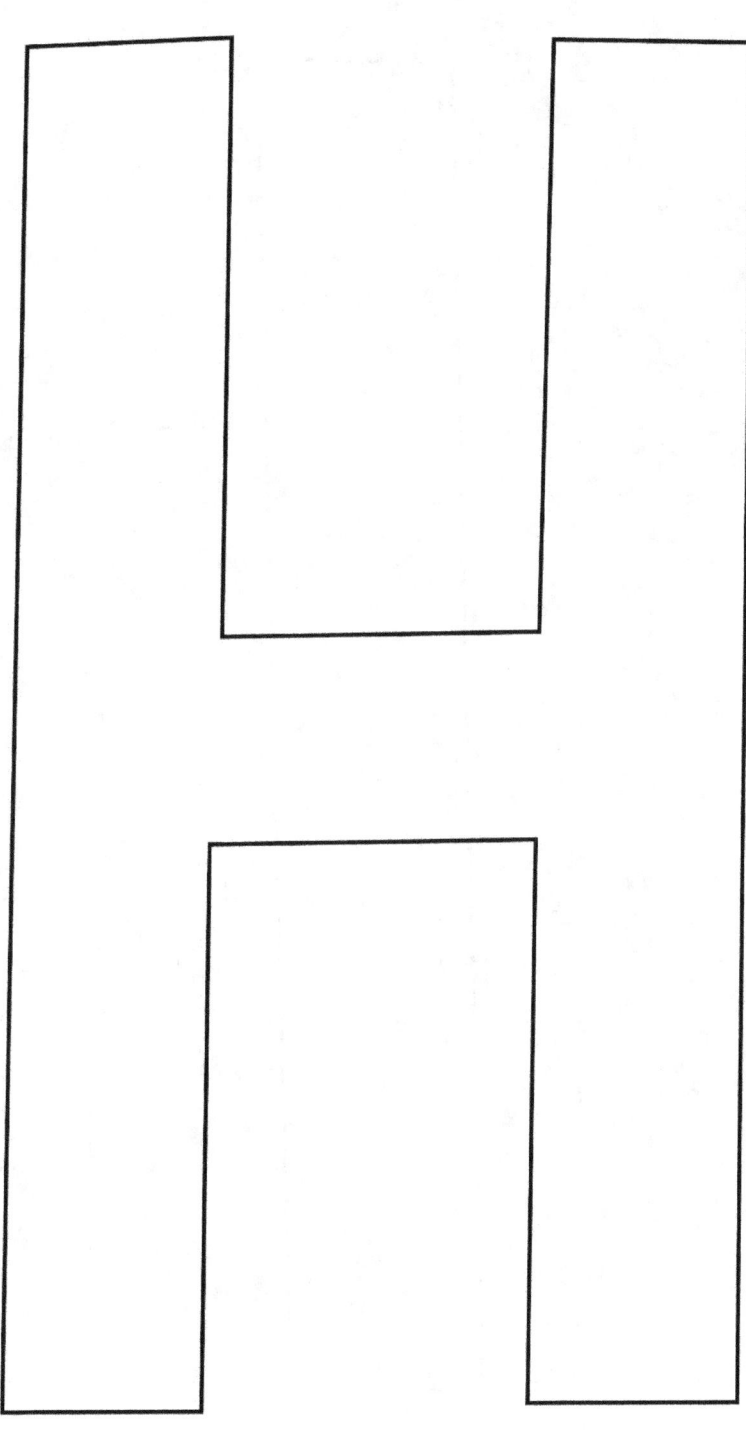

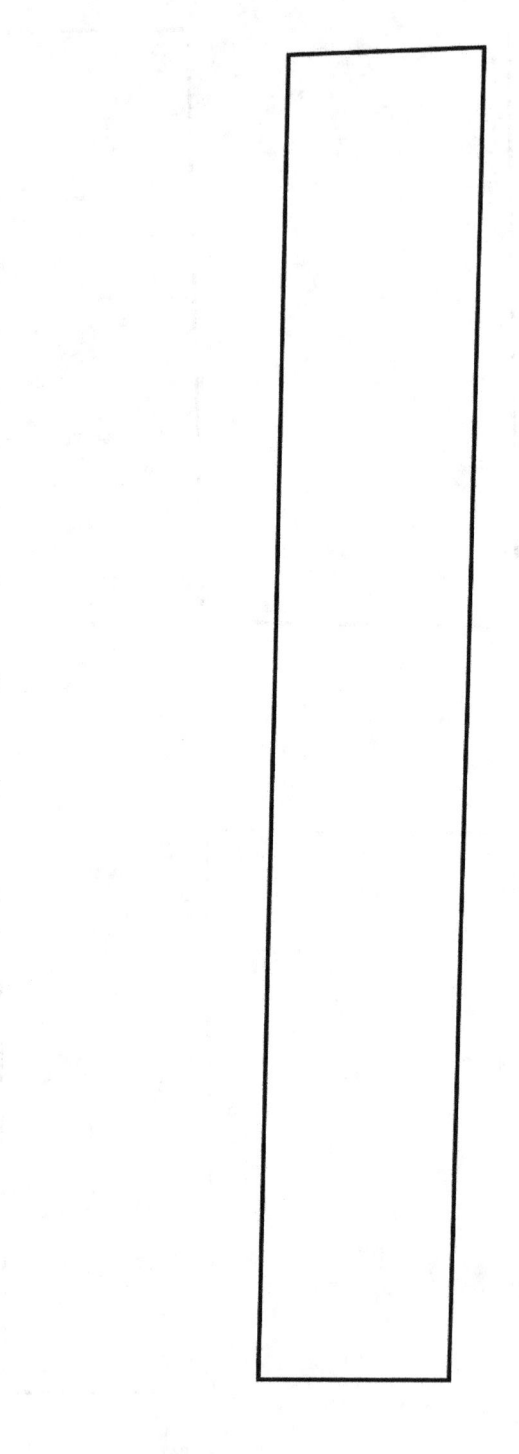

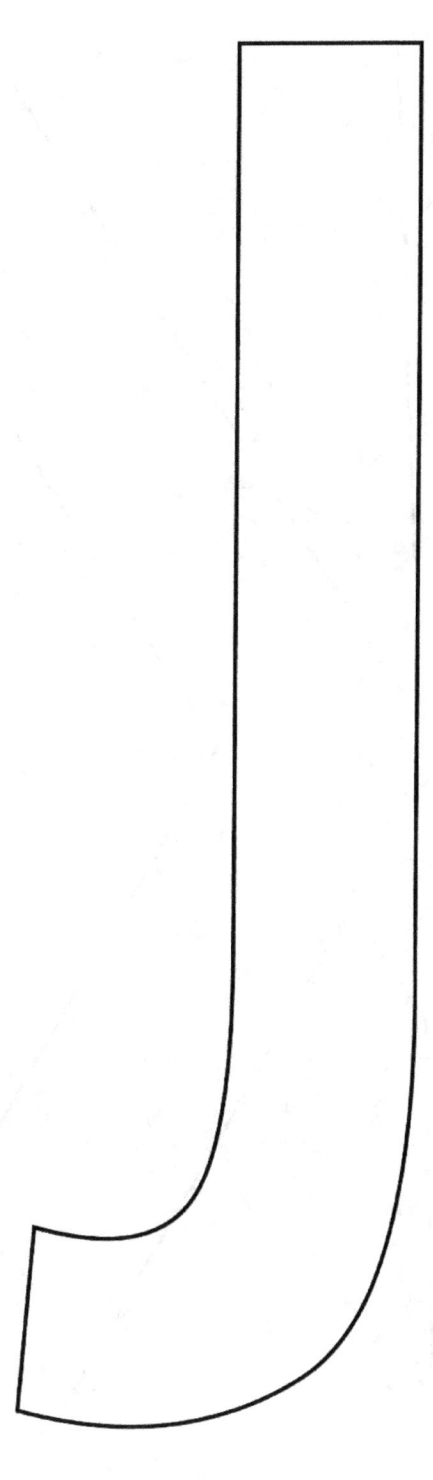

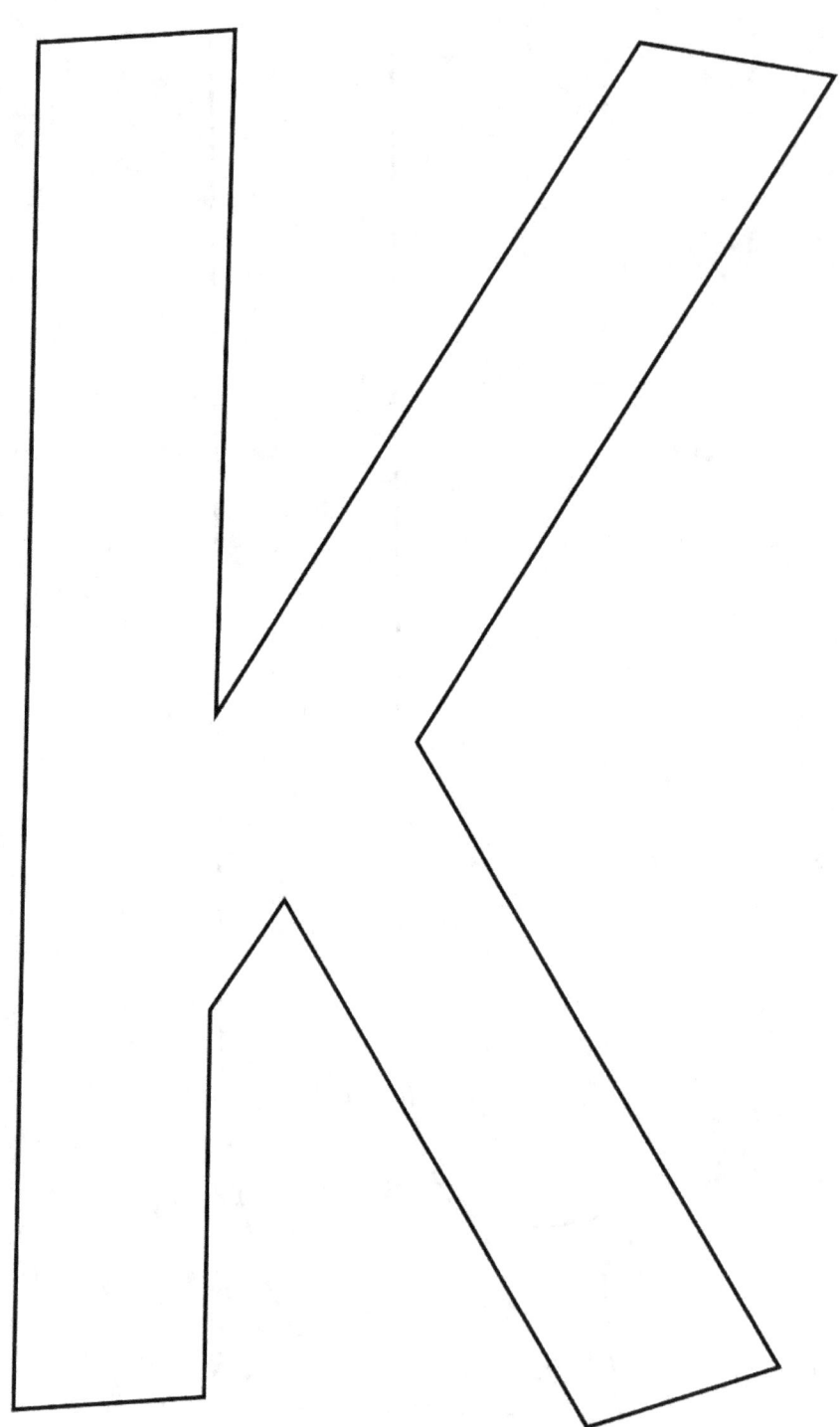

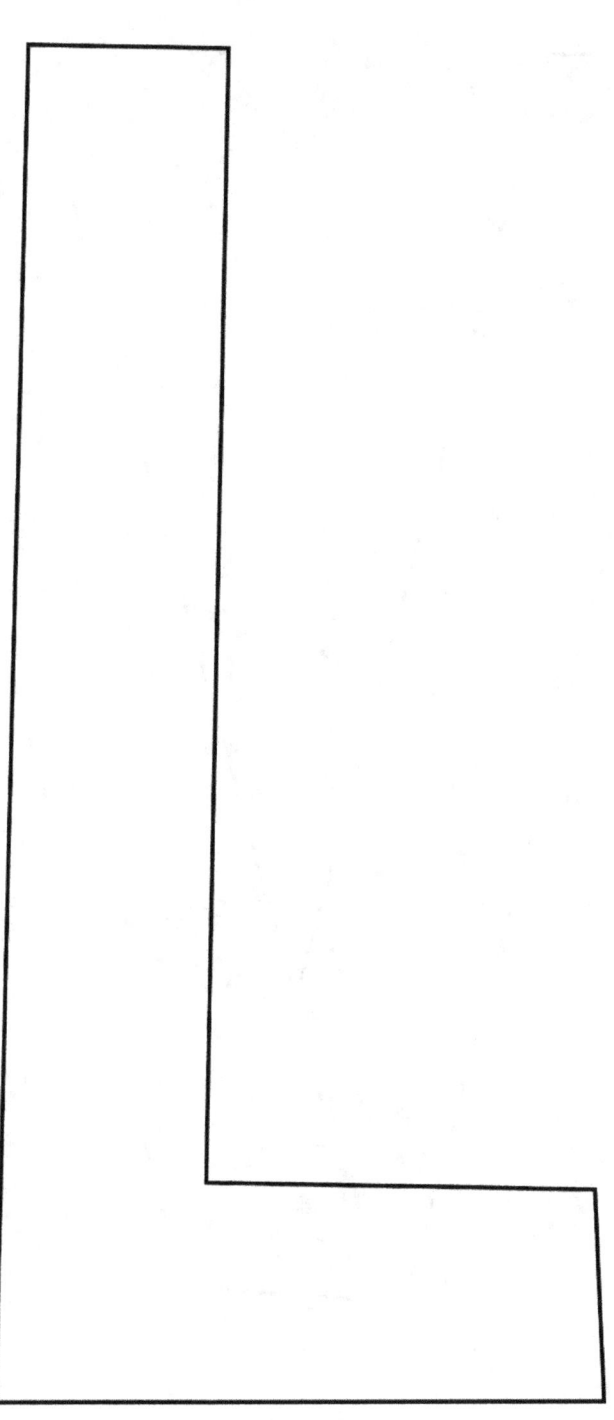

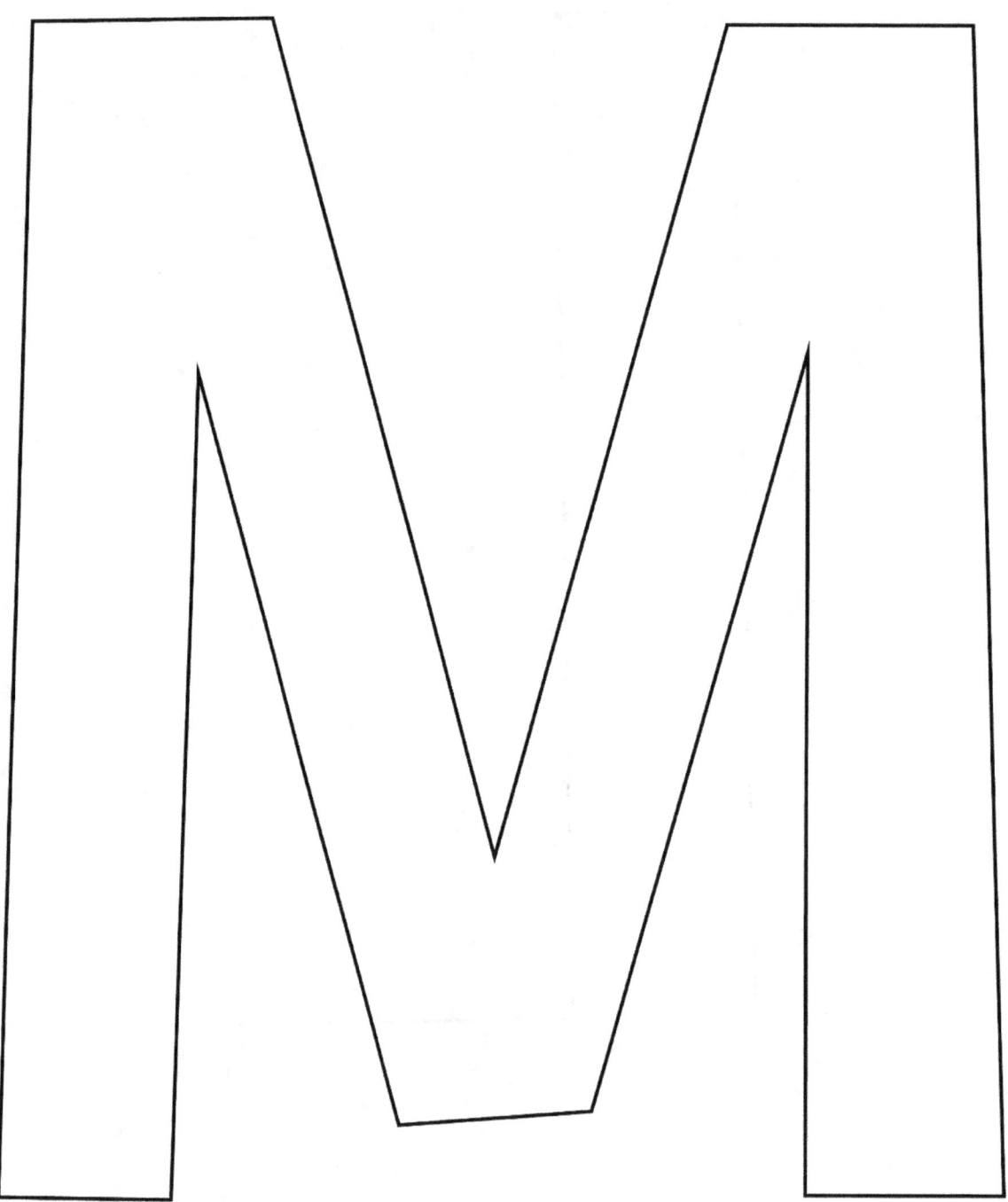

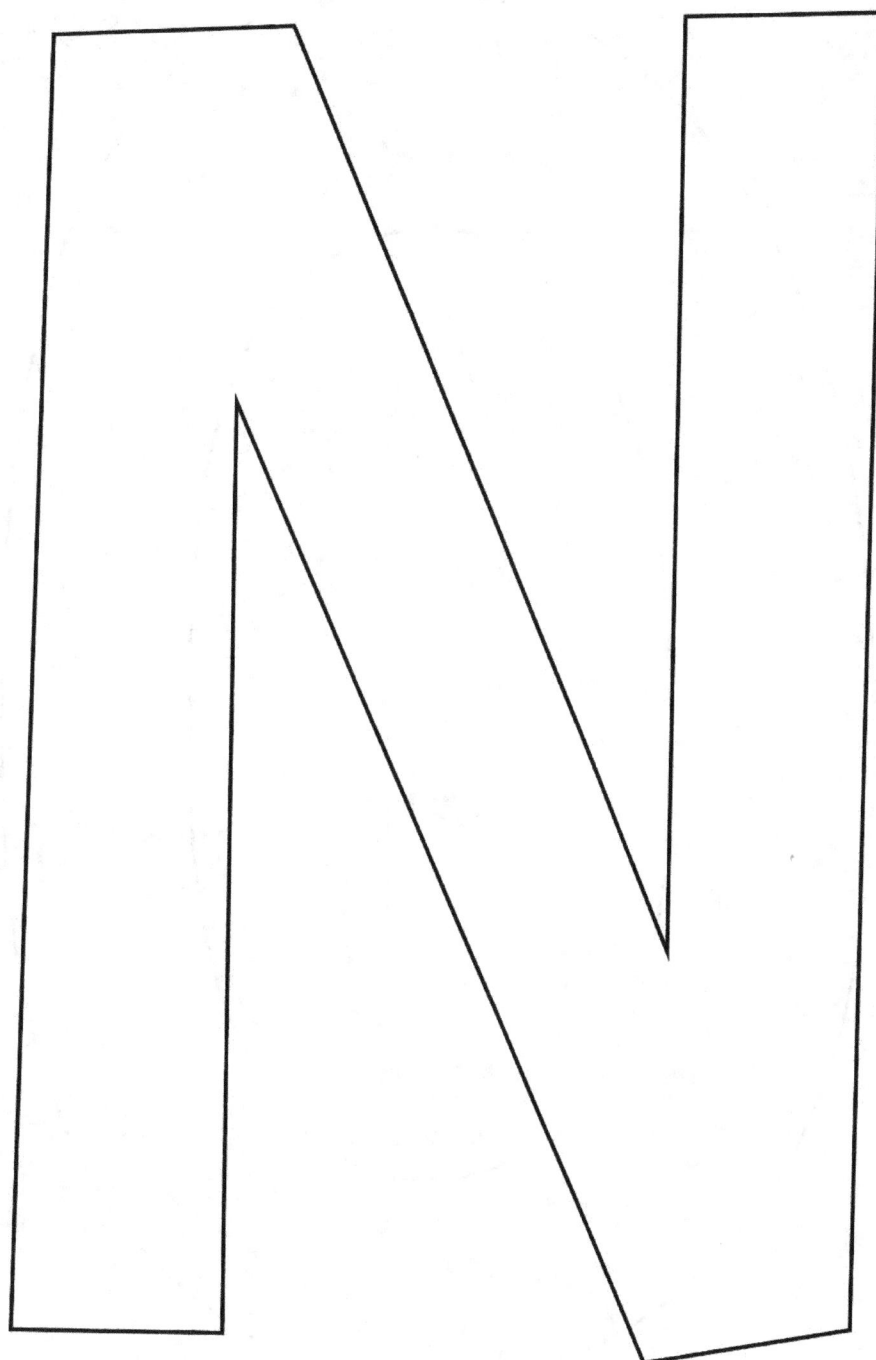

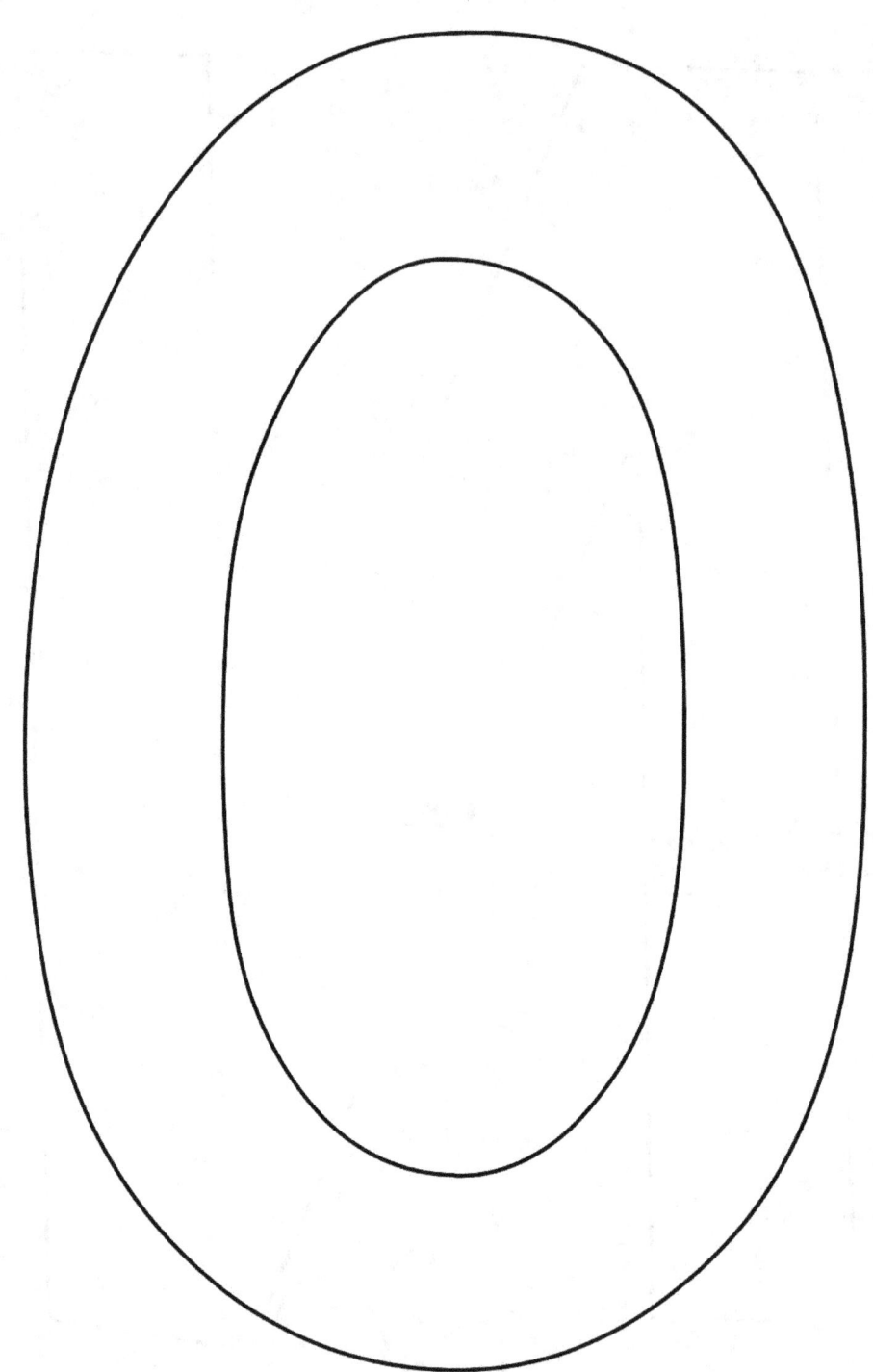

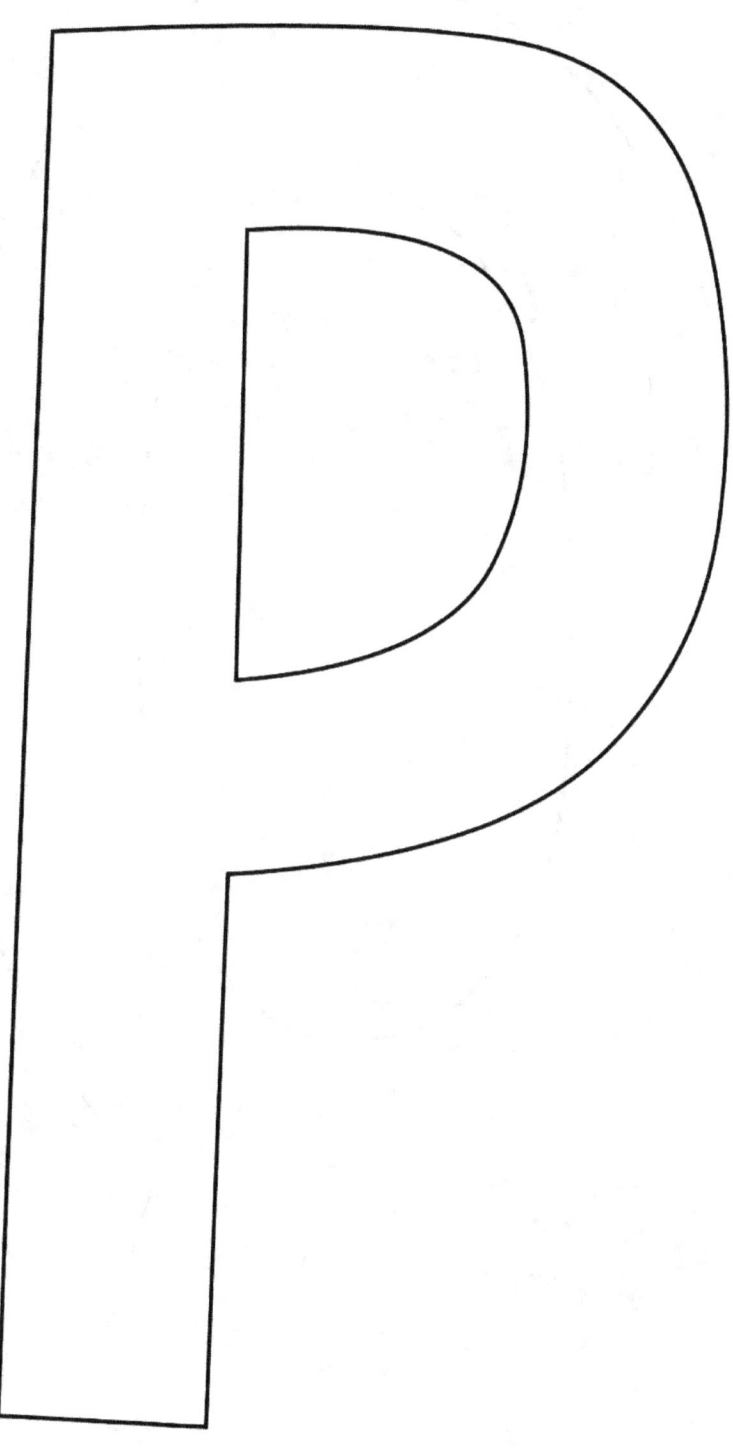

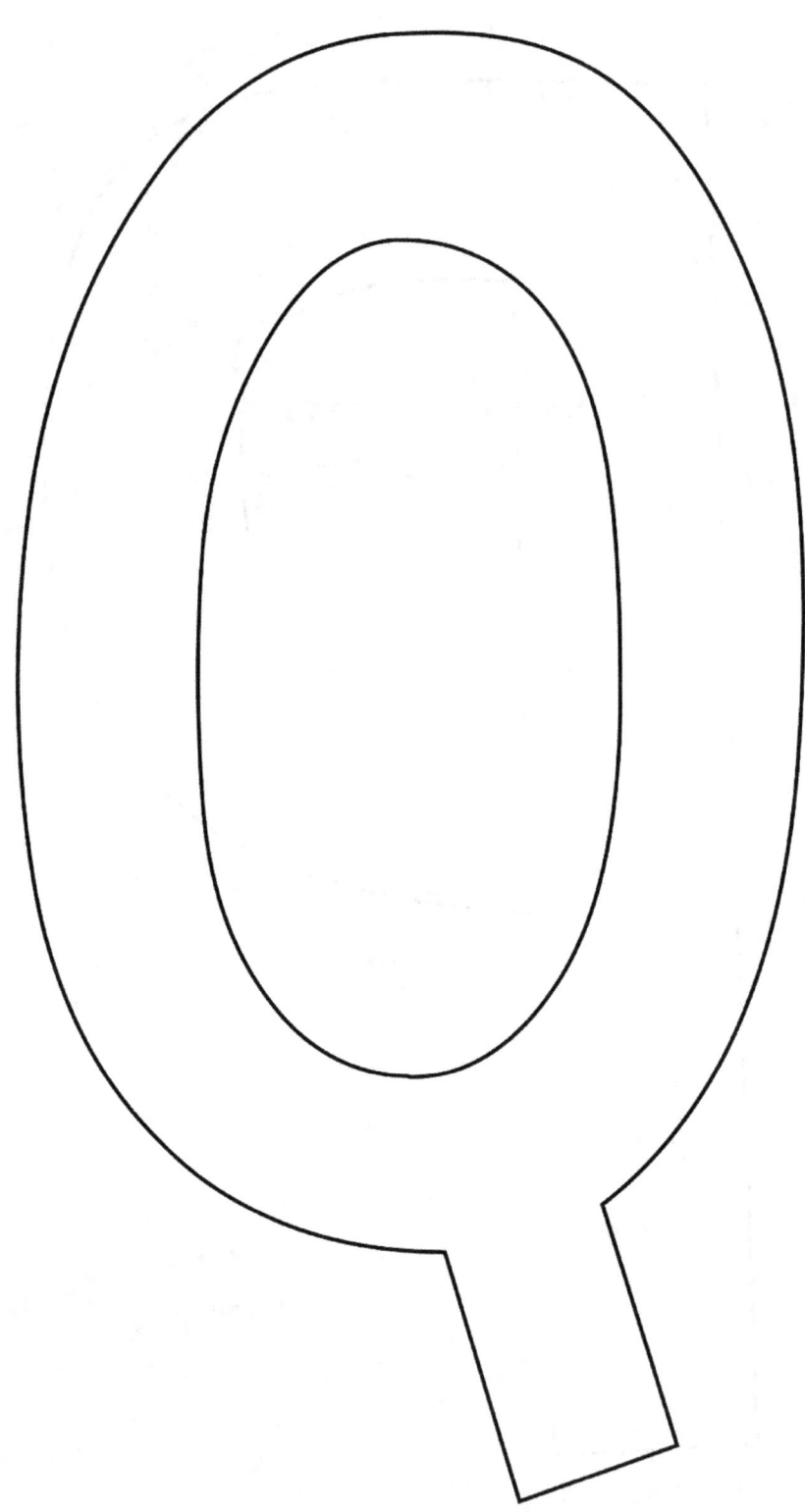

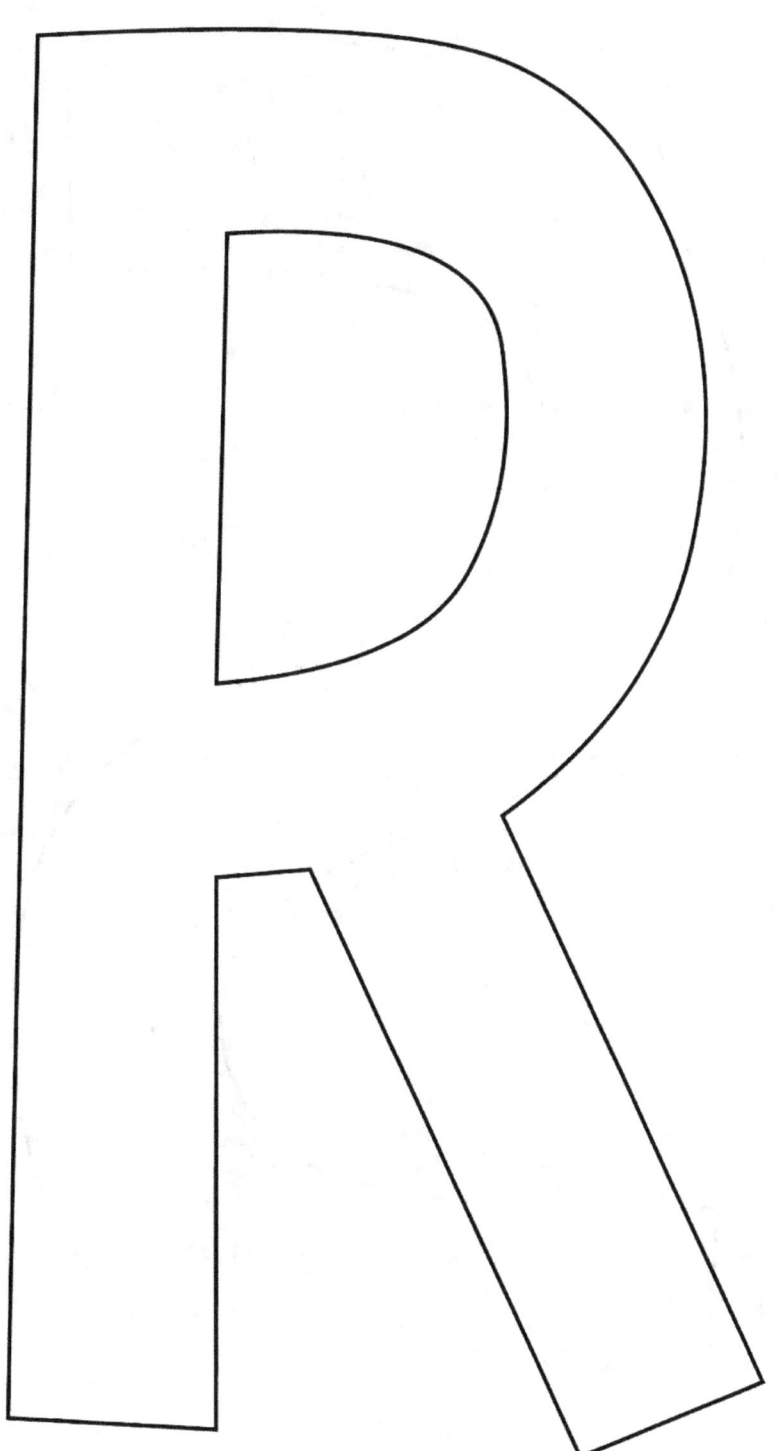

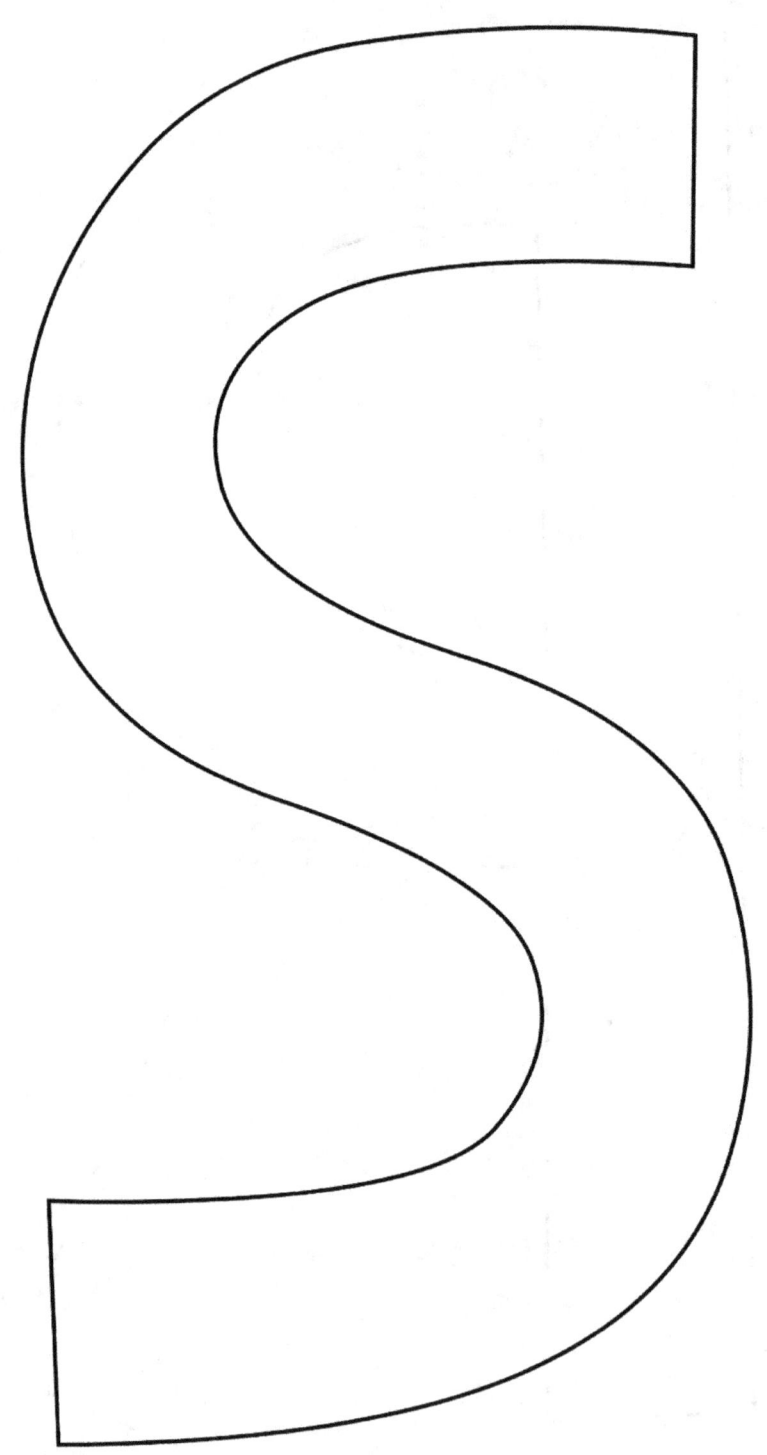

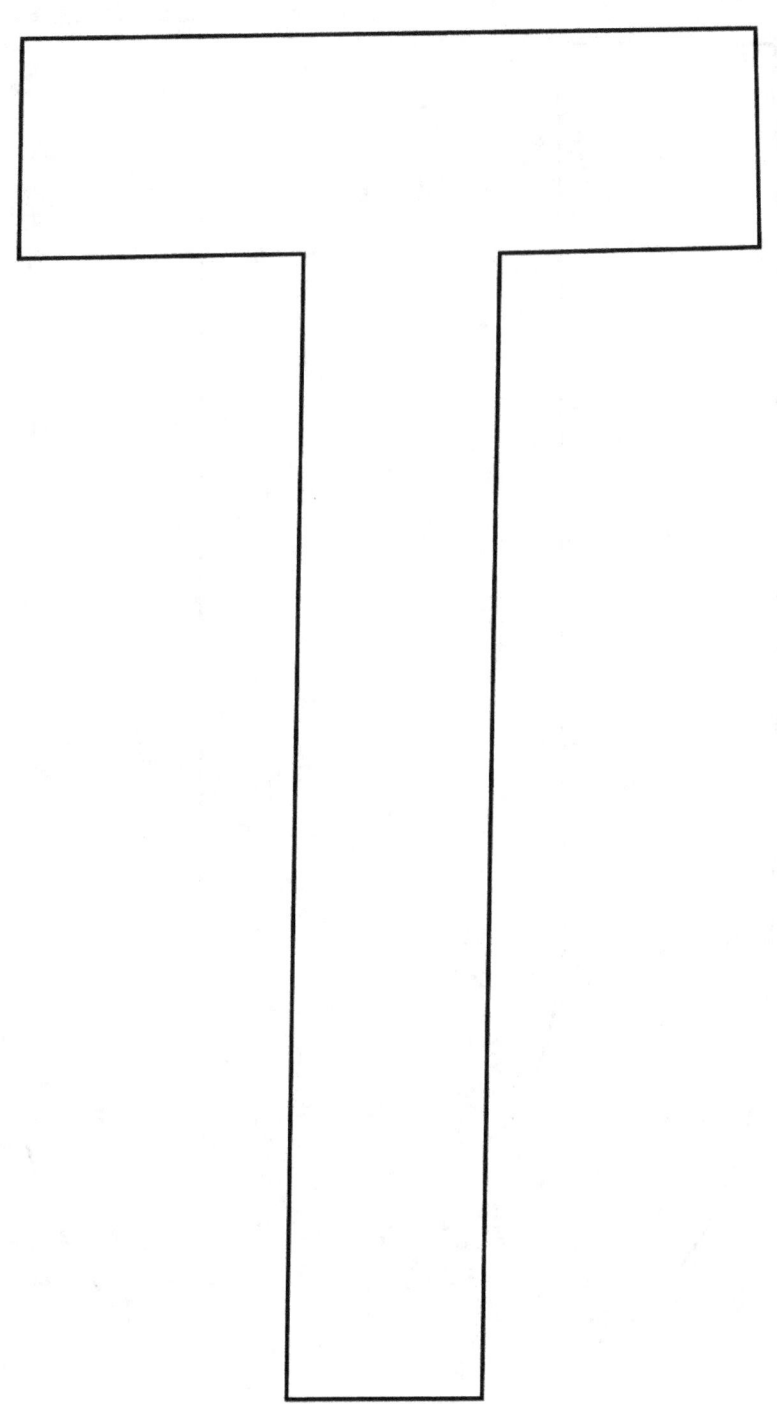

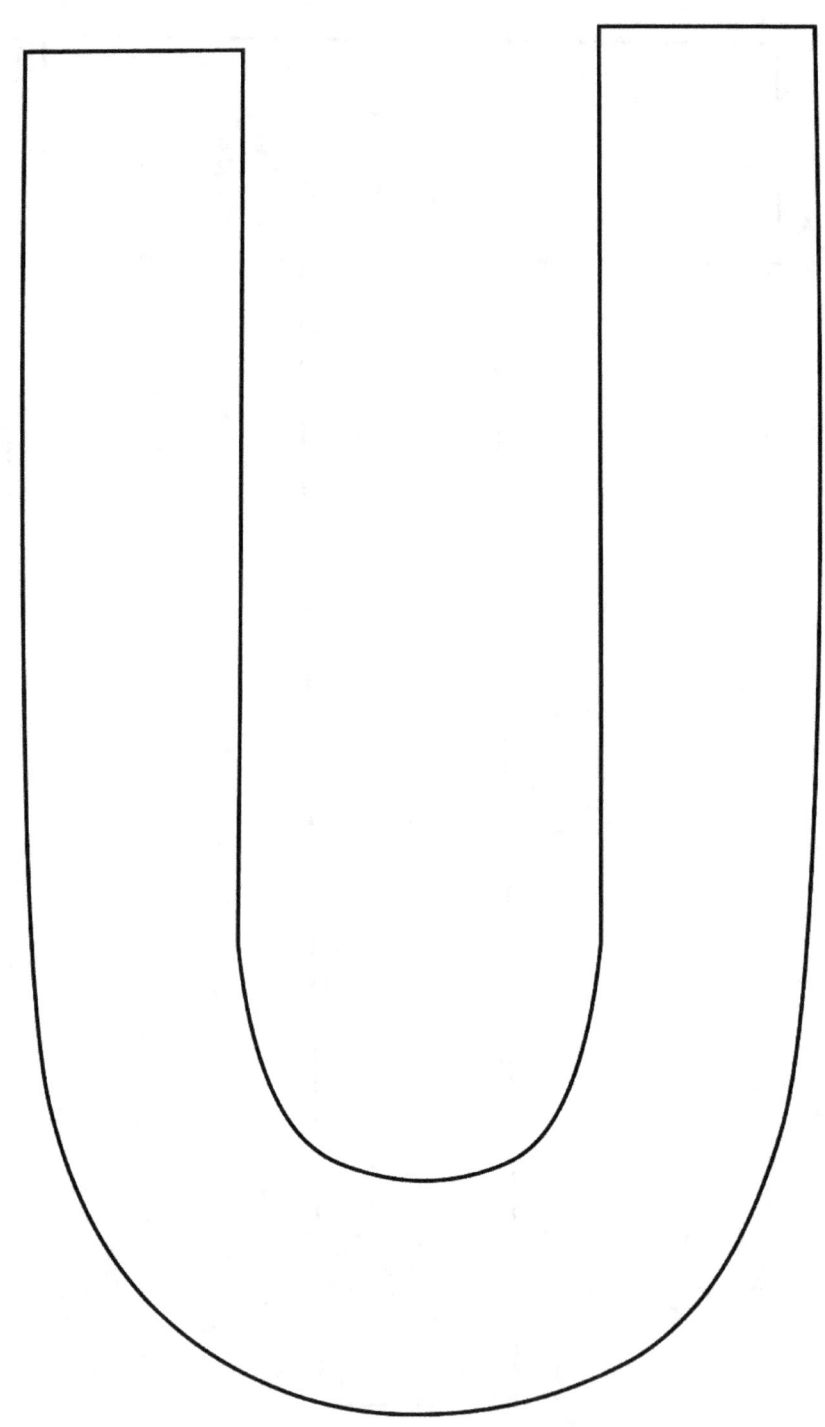

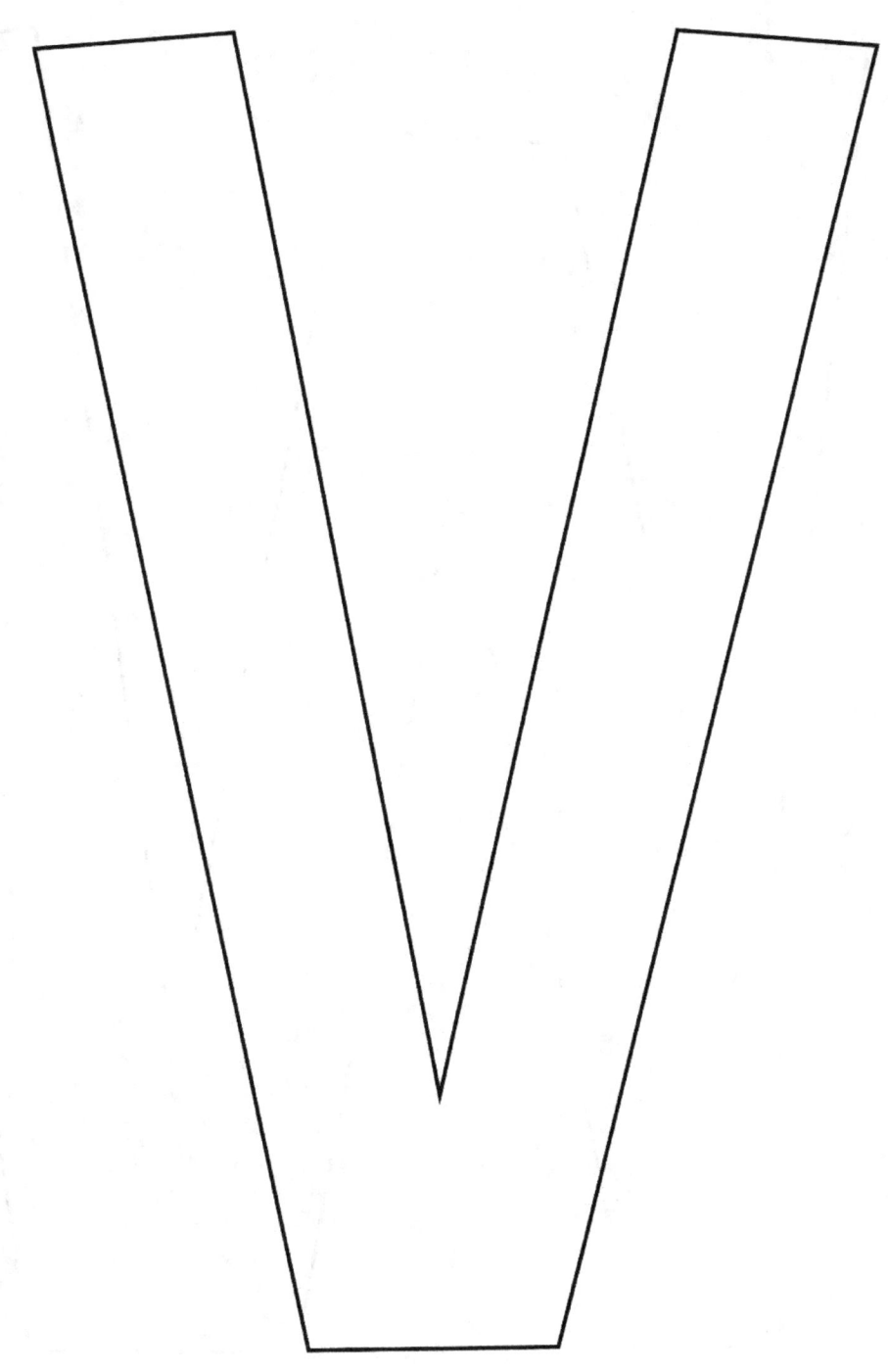

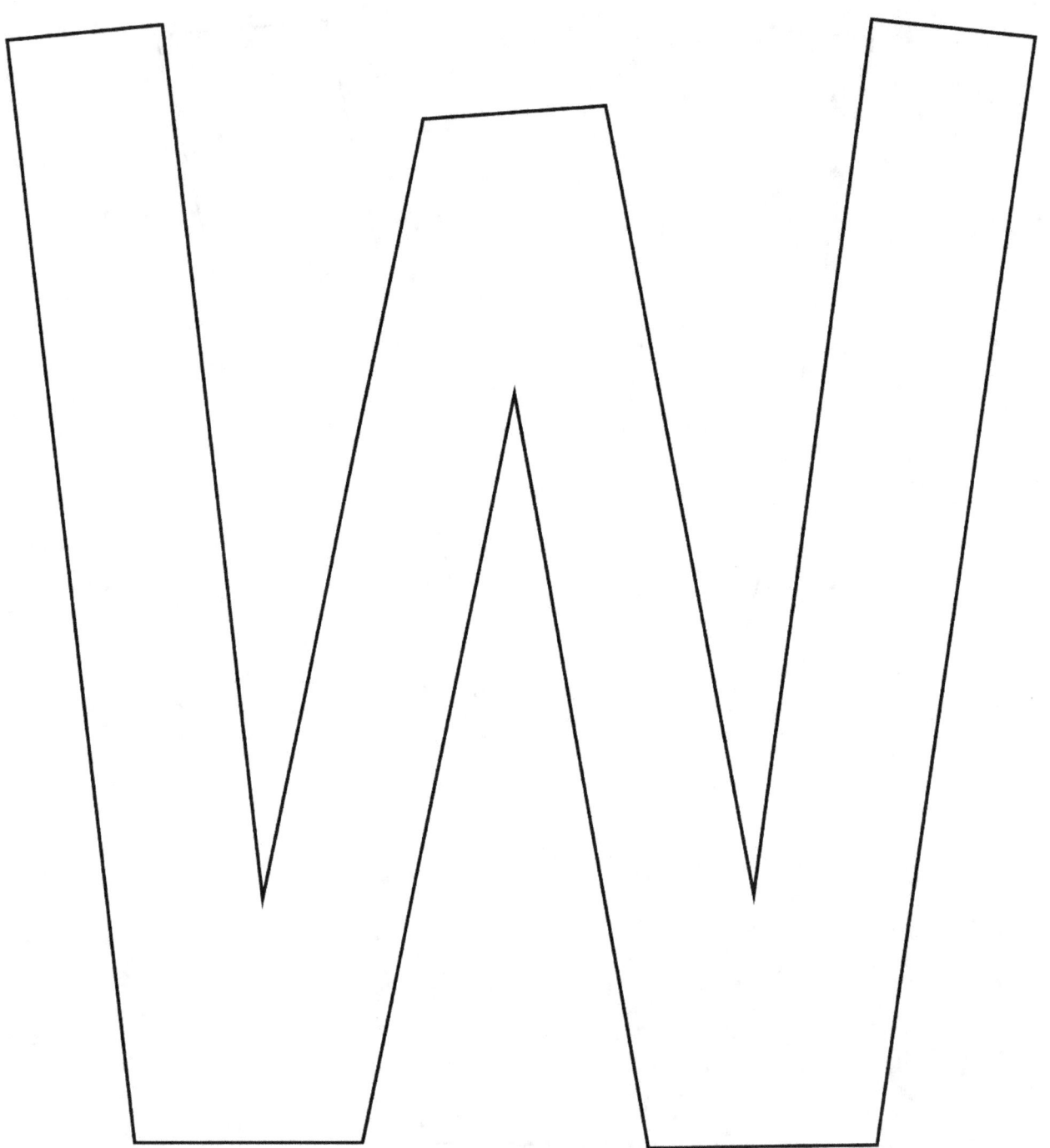

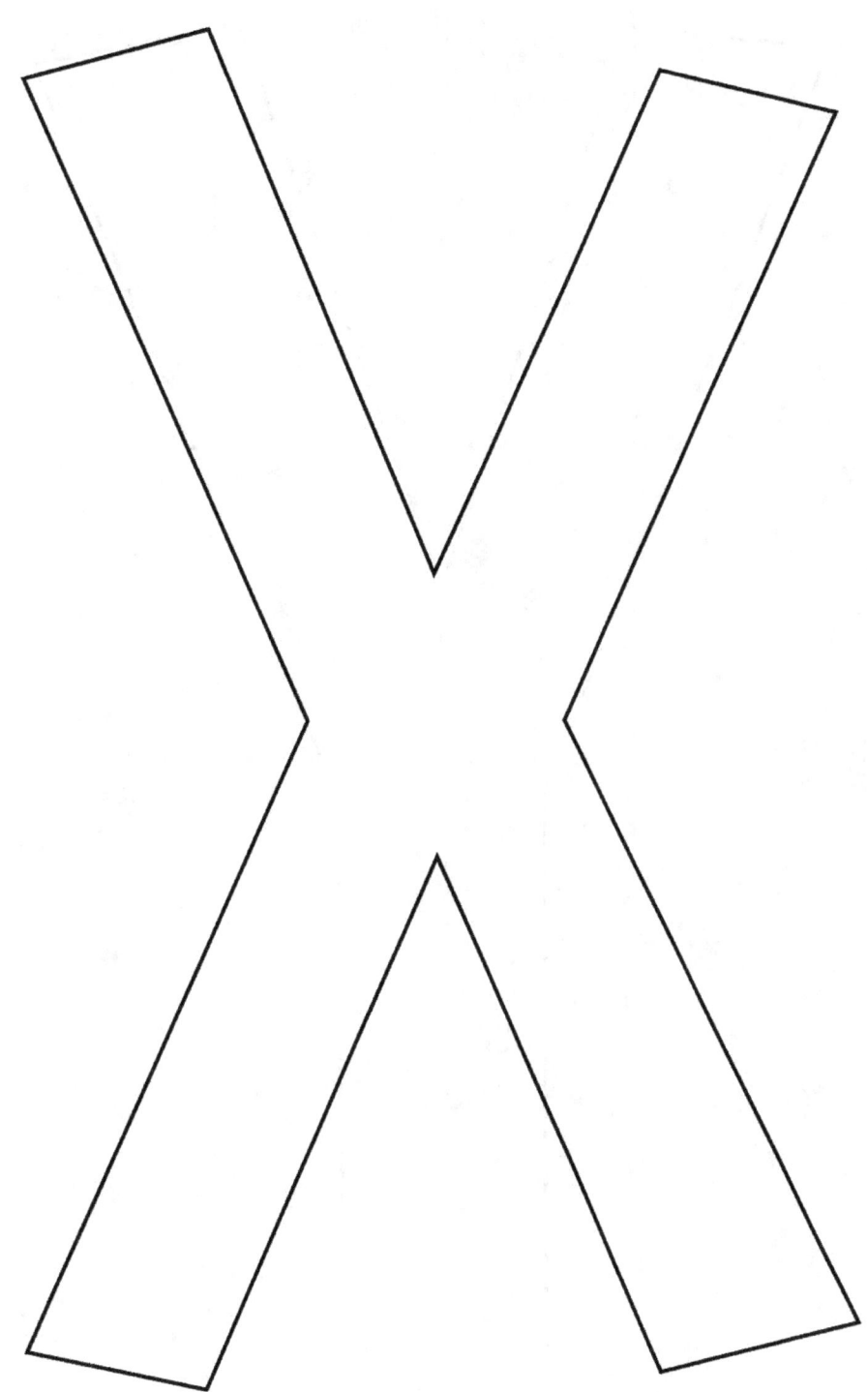

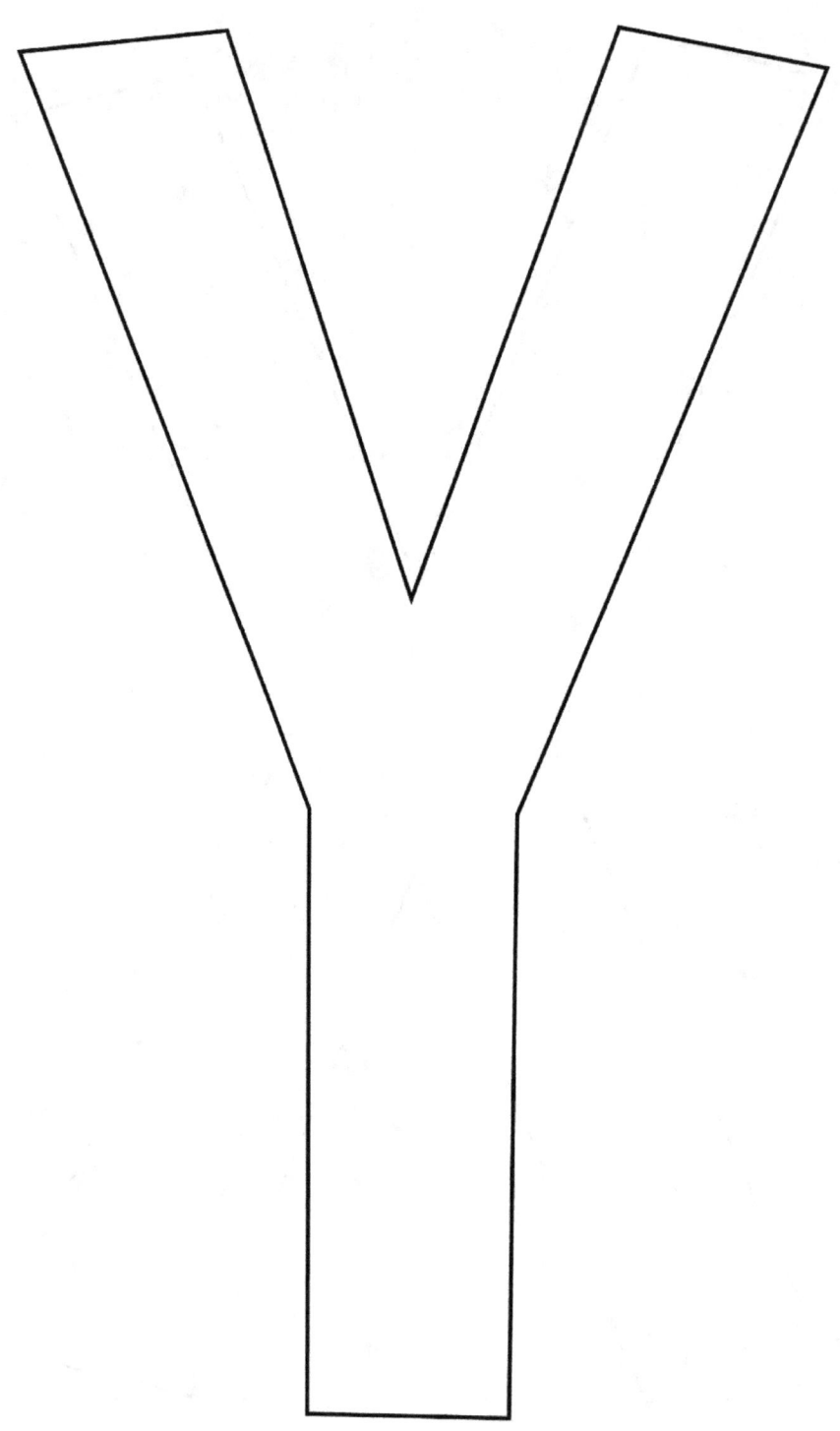

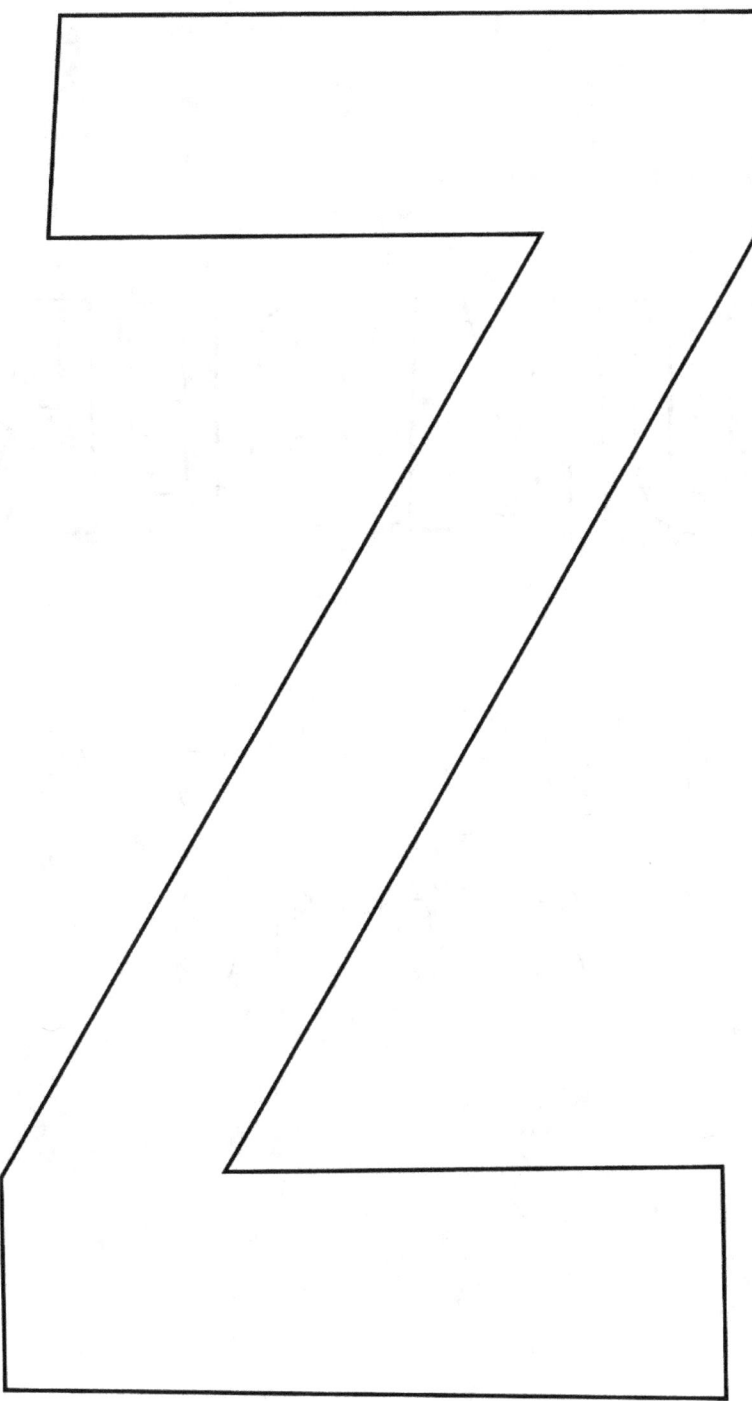

NUMBERS

0 1 2 3 4 5 6 7 8 9 10

0

ZERO

1

ONE

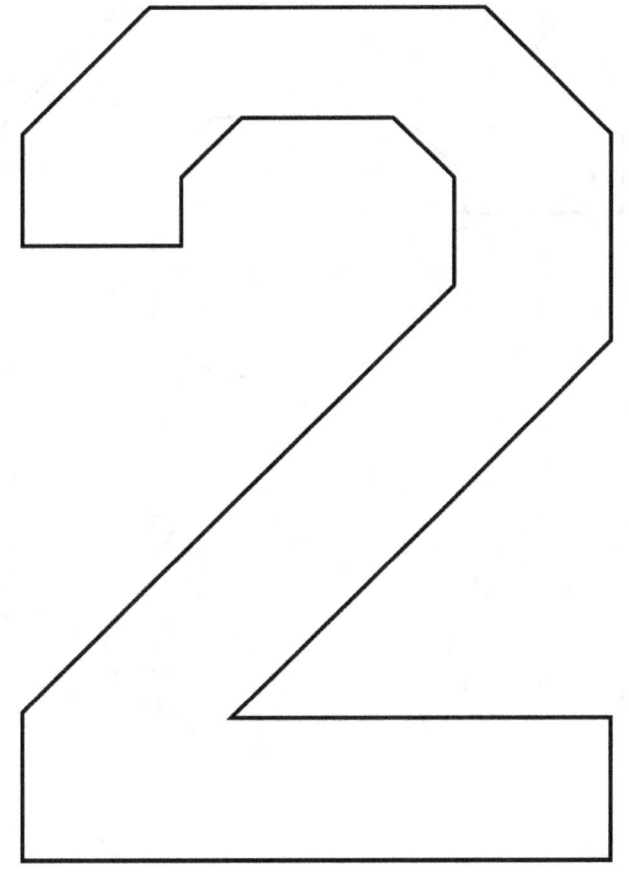

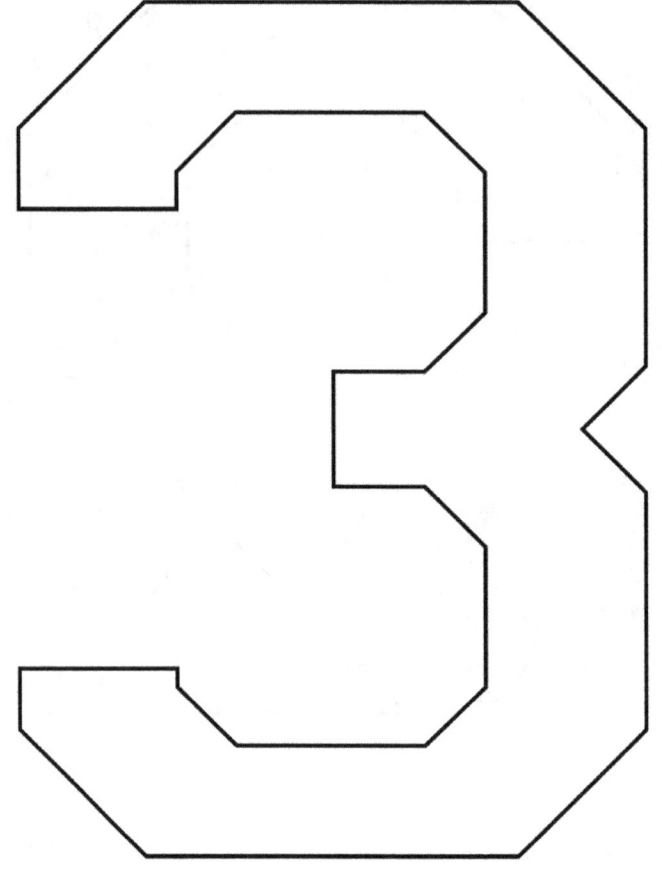

3

THREE

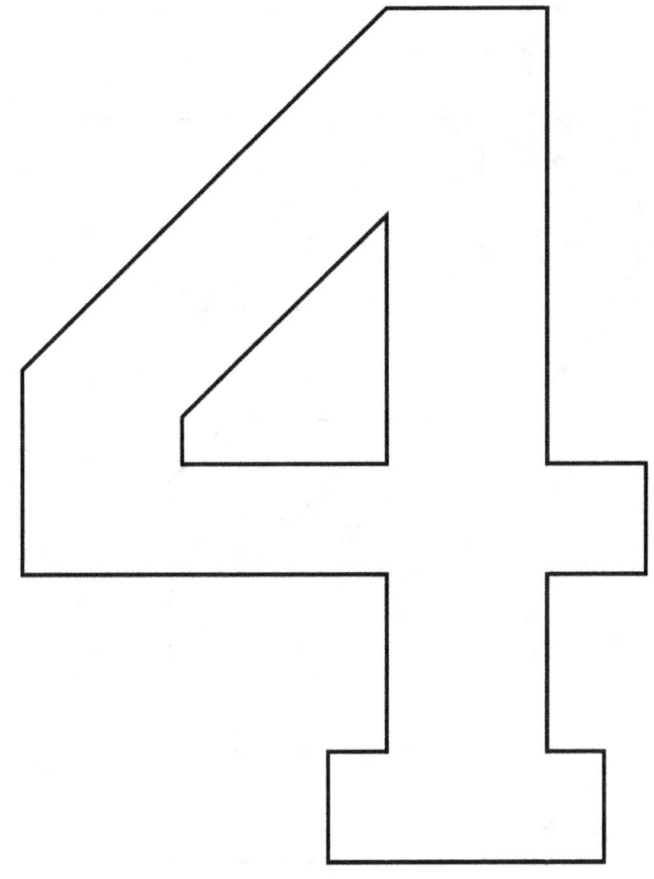

FOUR

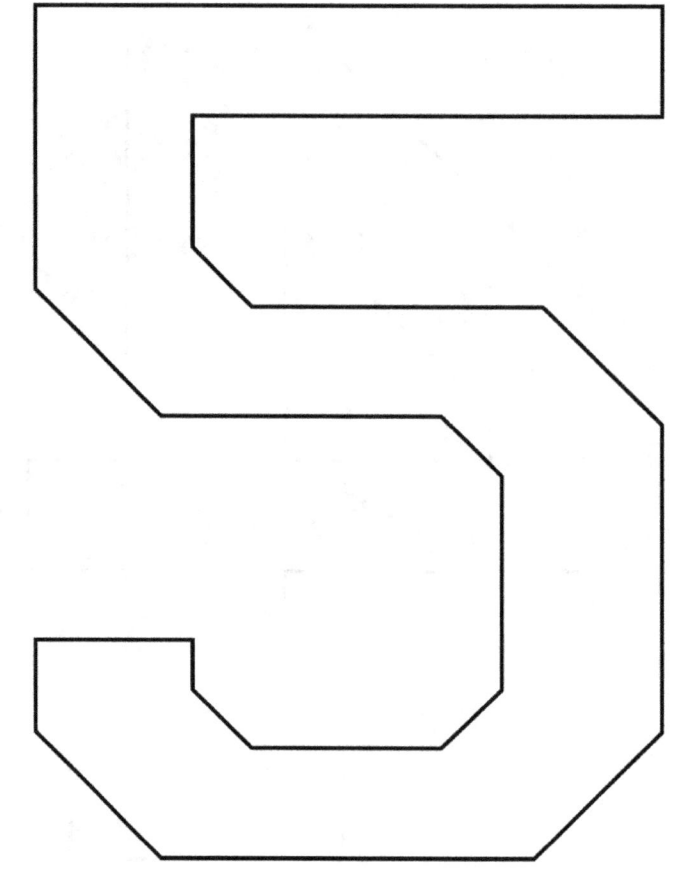

FIVE

6

SIX

7

SEVEN

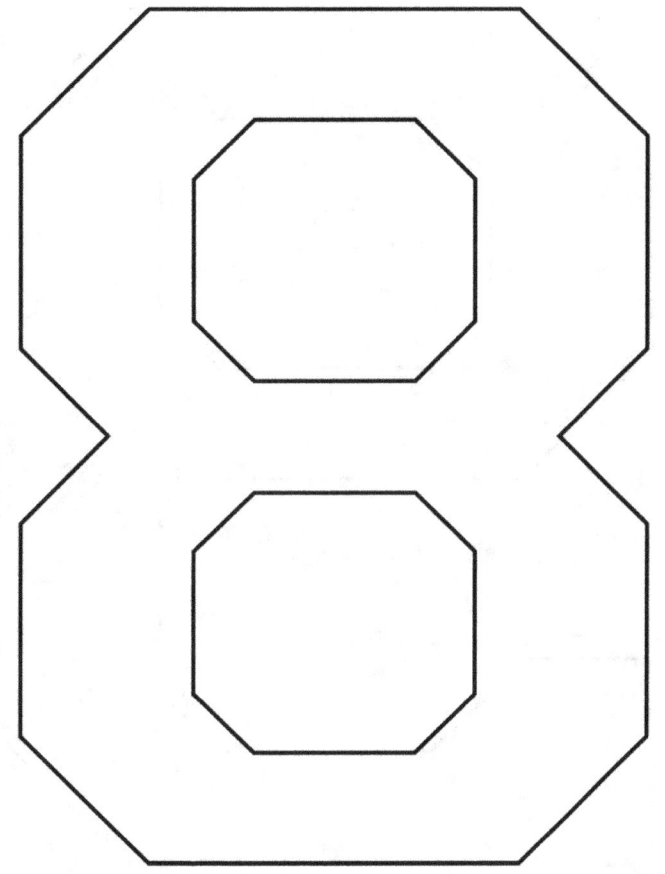

EIGHT

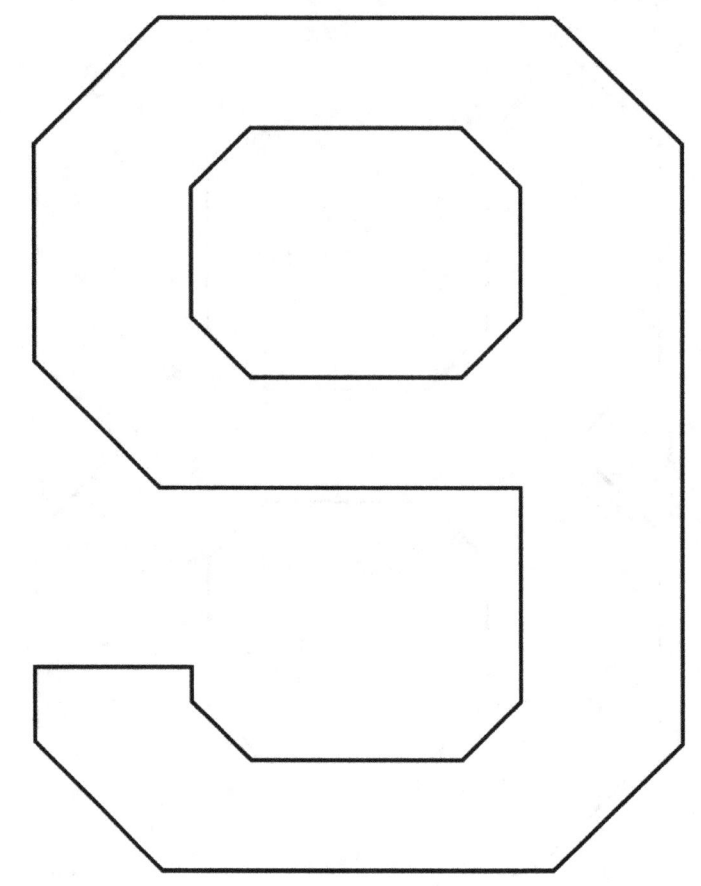

9 NINE

10

TEN

SHAPES

SQUARE

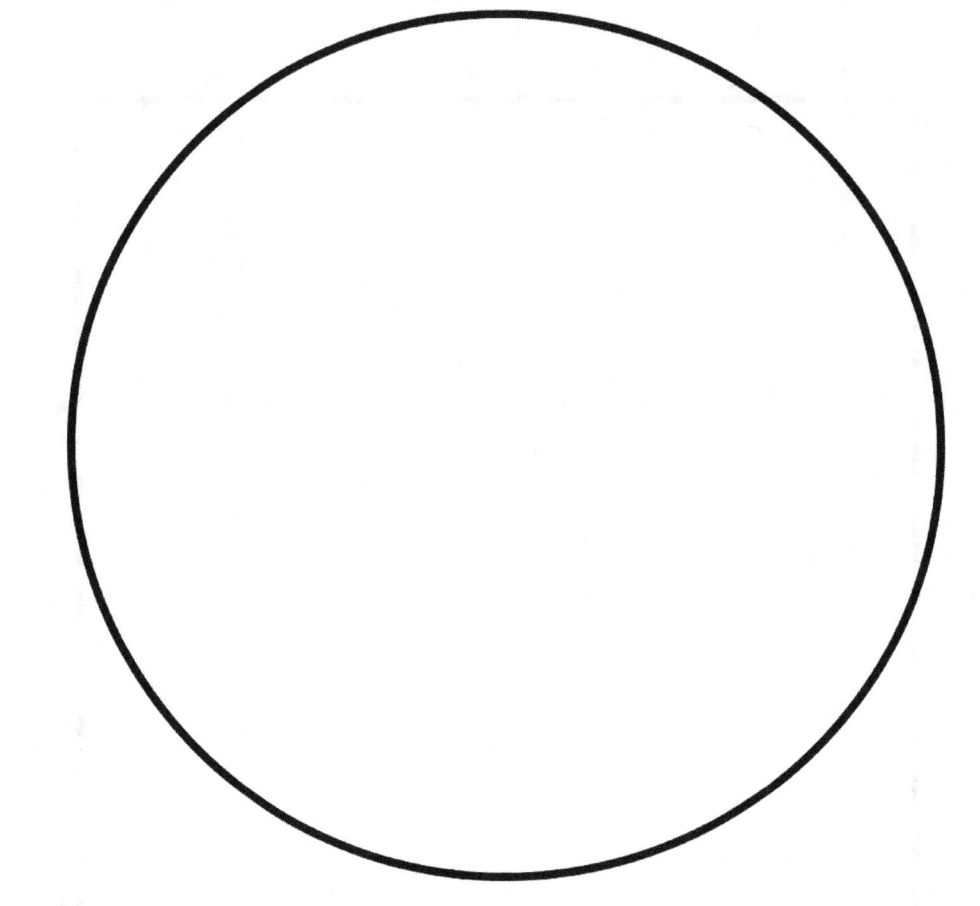

CIRCLE

HEART

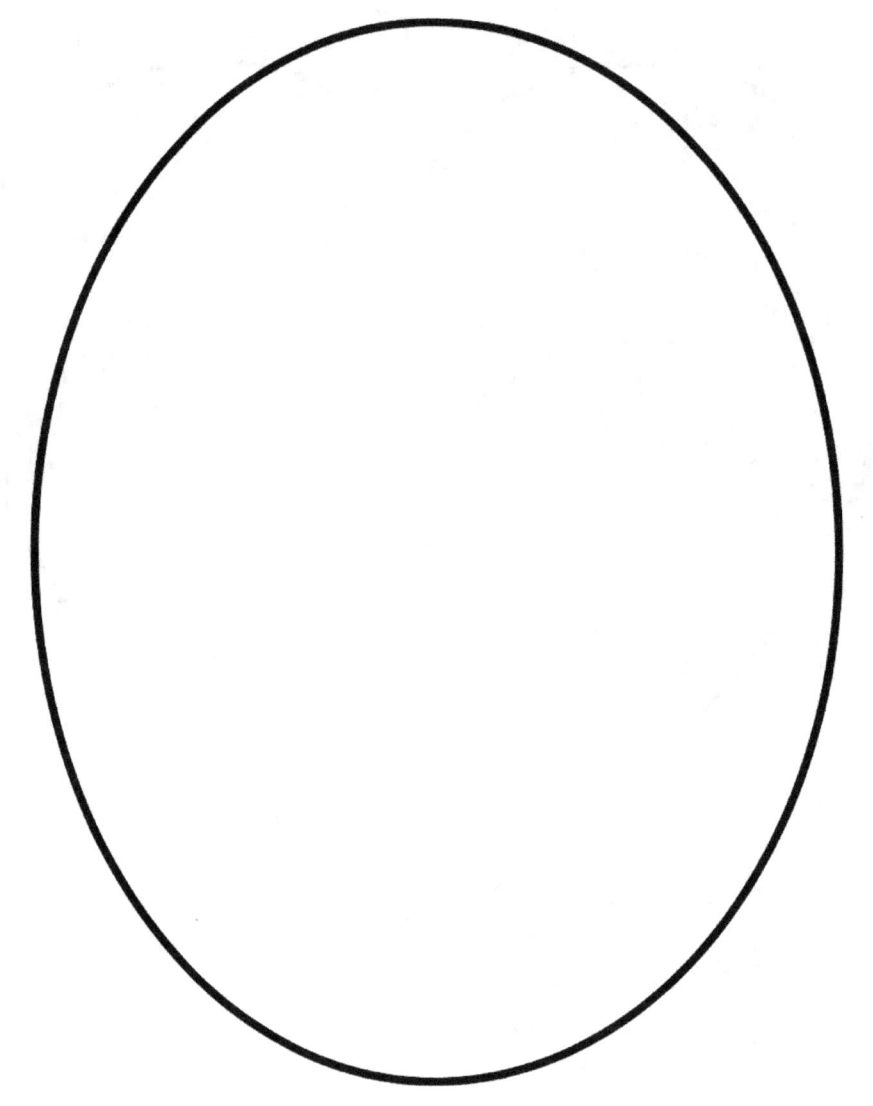

ELLIPSE

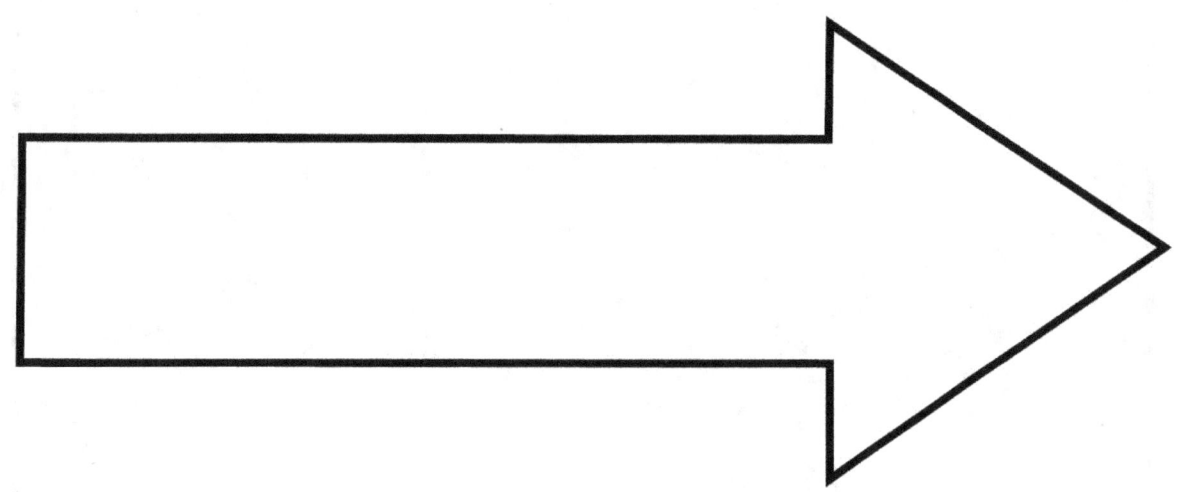

ARROW

RECTANGLE

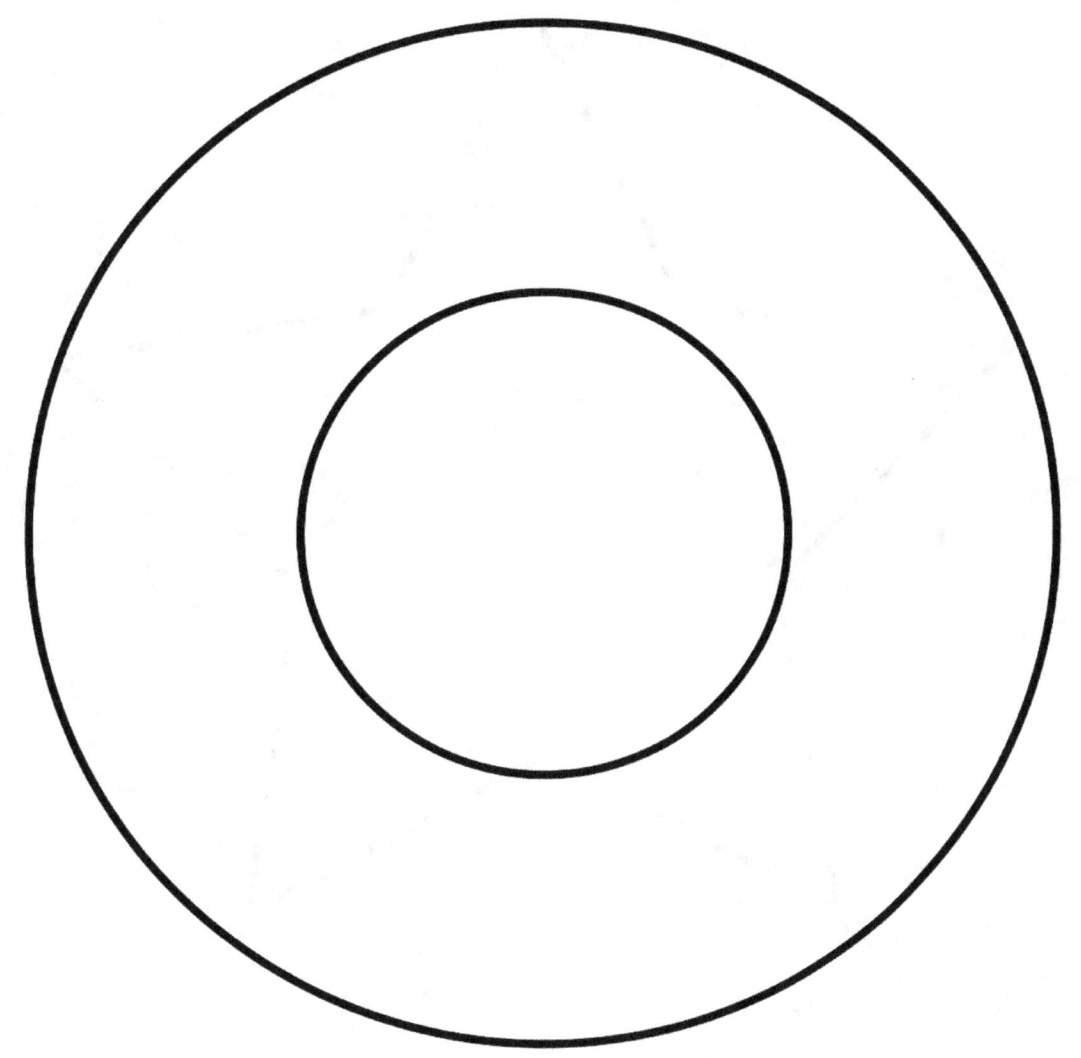

RINGE

STAR

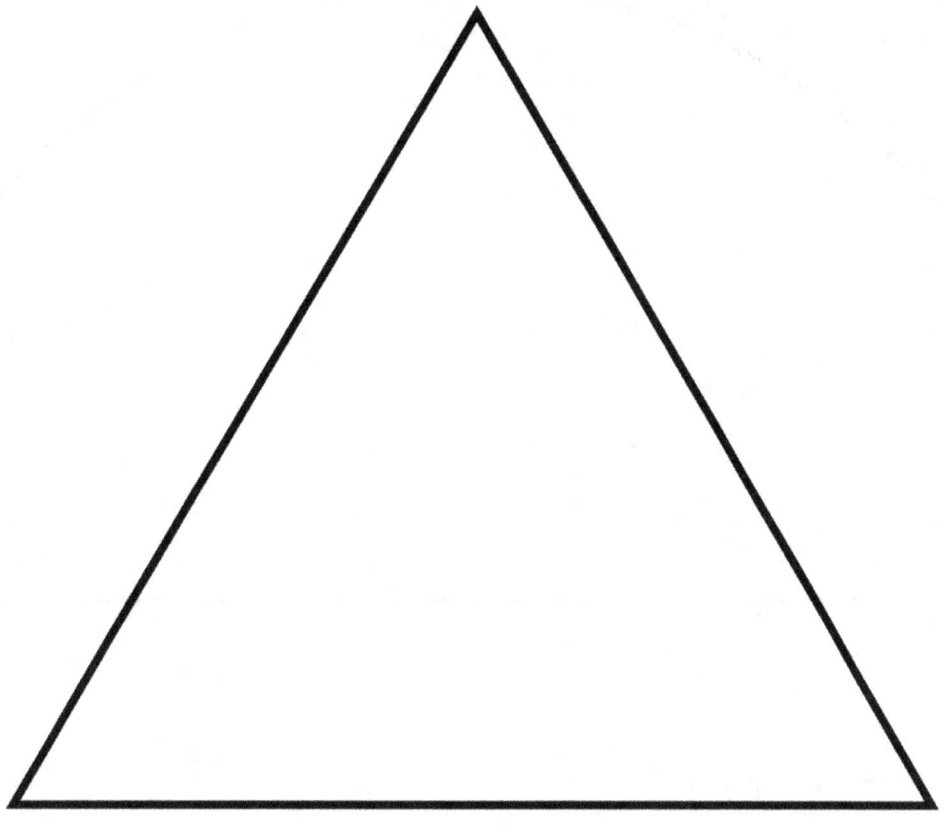

TRIANGLE

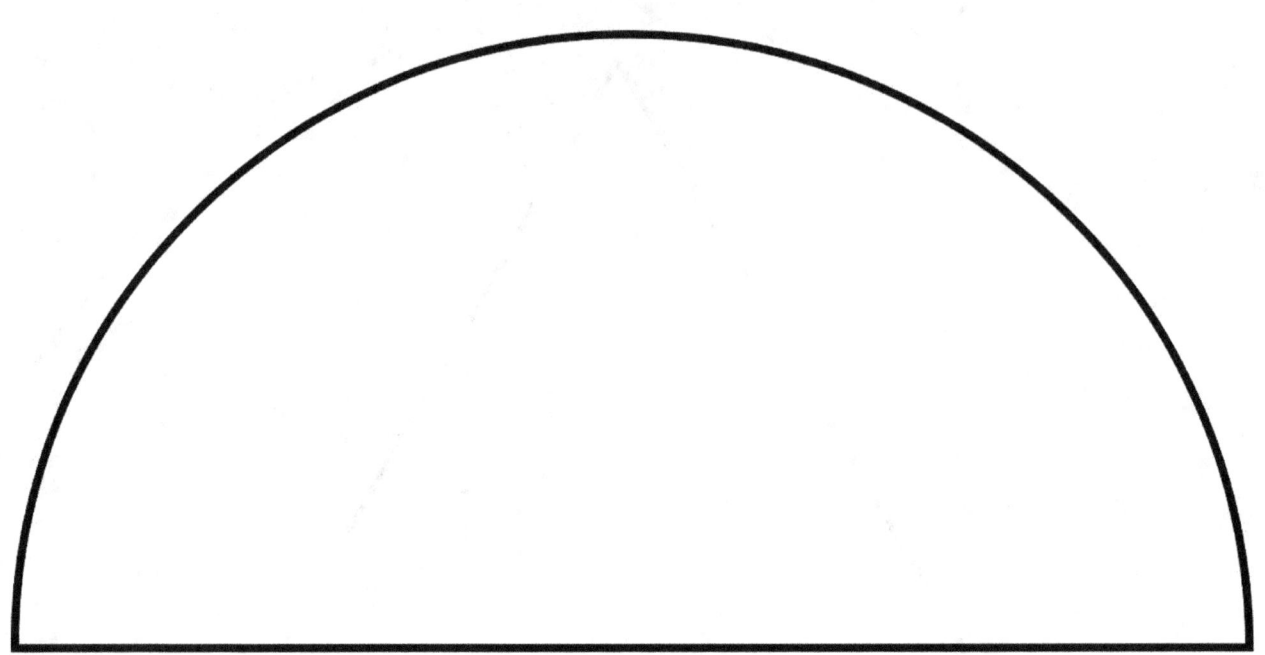

SEMICIRCLE

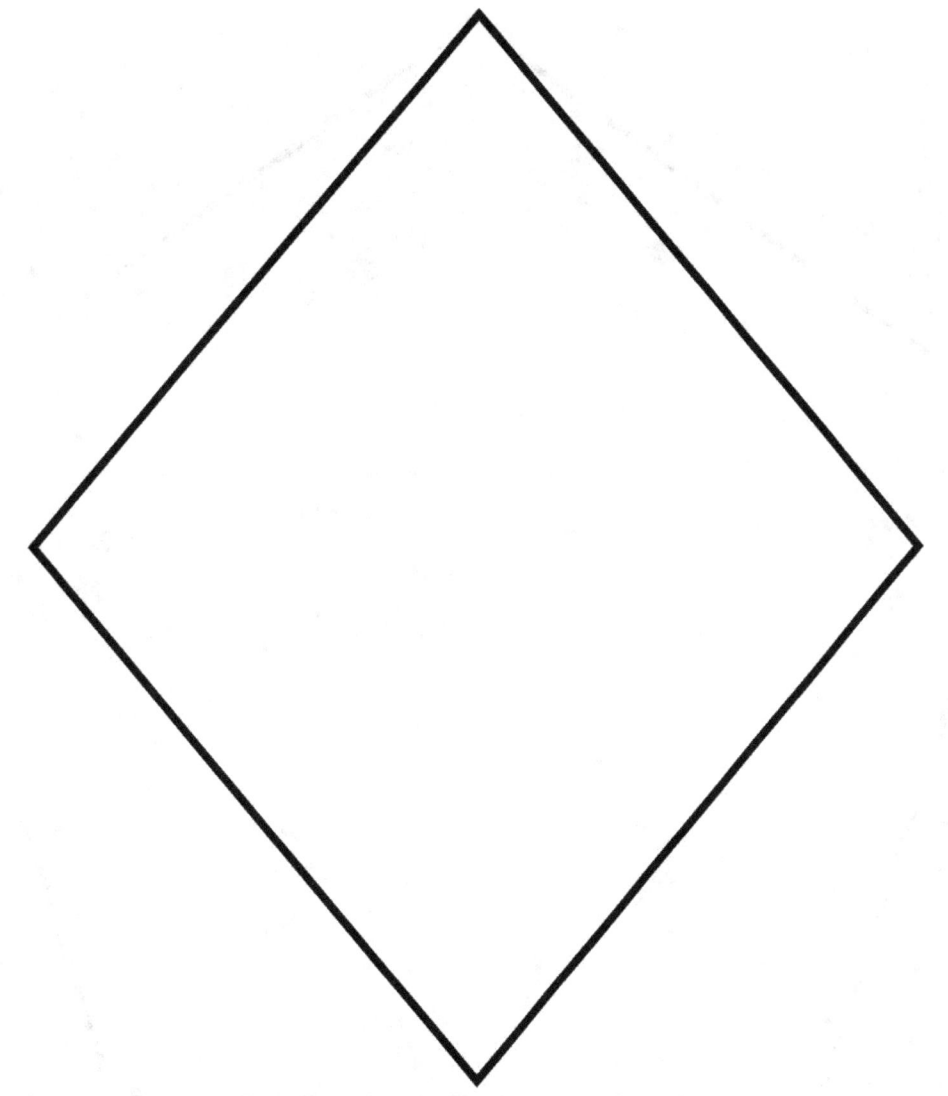

RHOMBUS

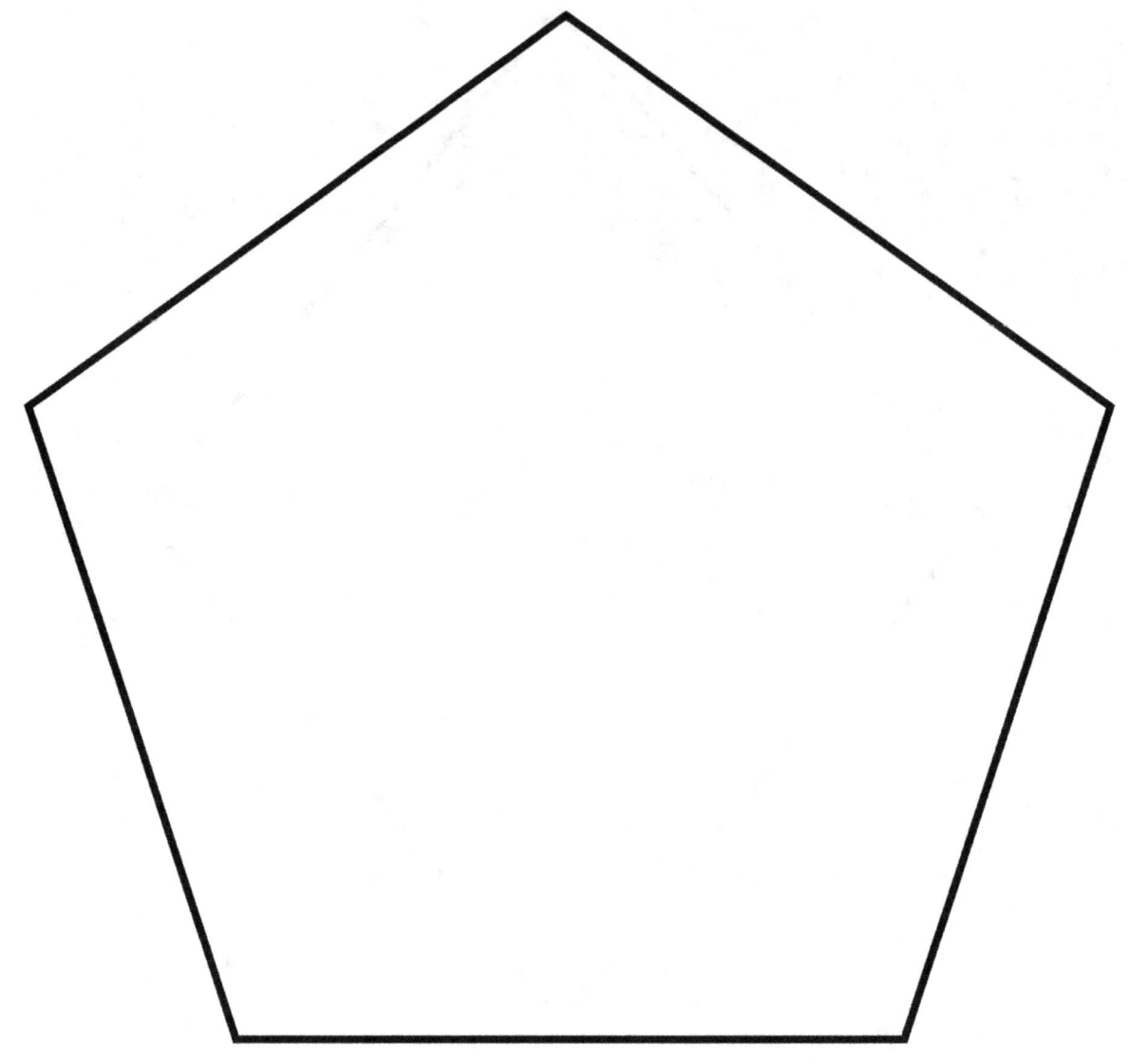

PENTAGON

ANIMALS

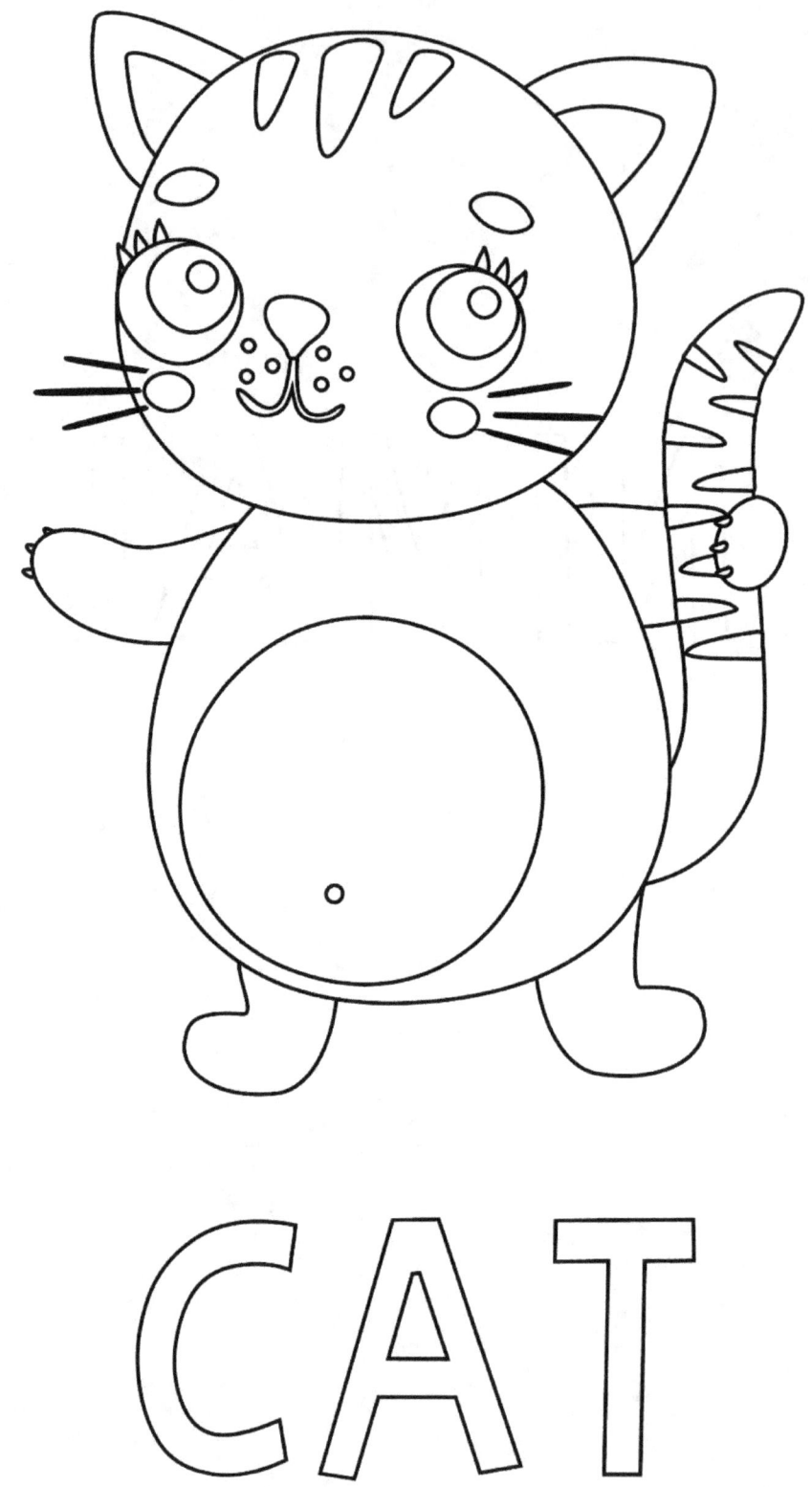

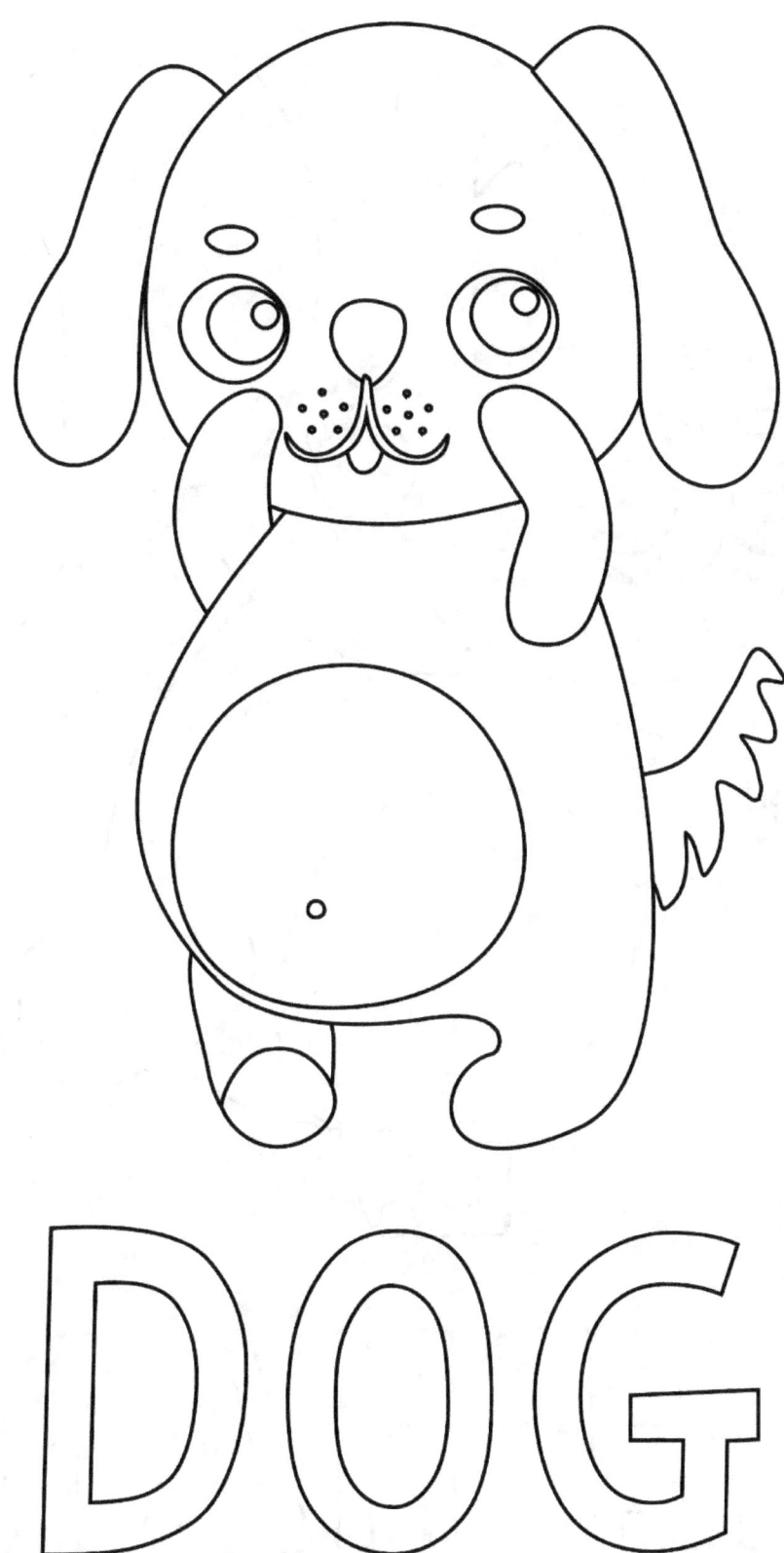

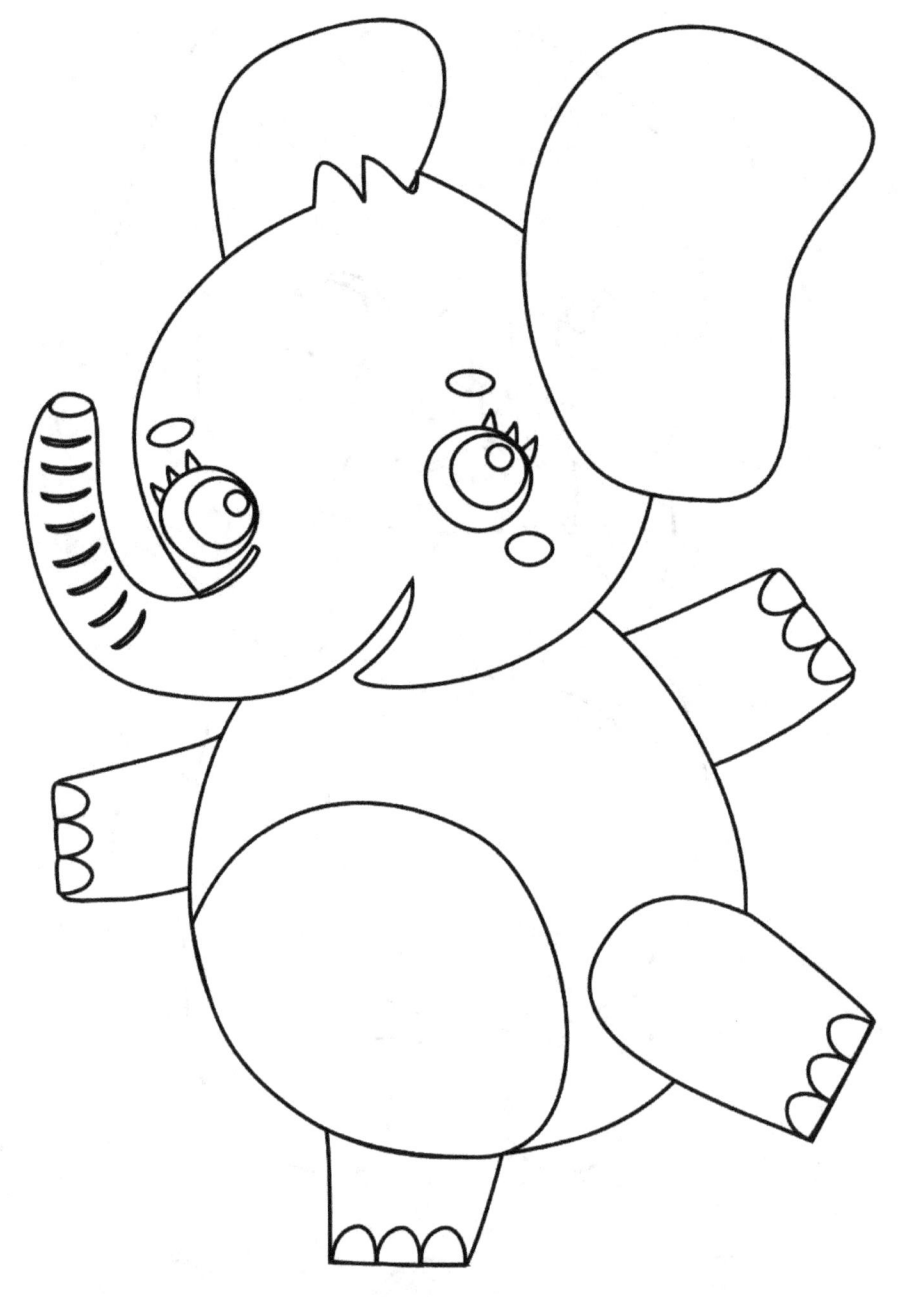

ELEPHANT

FOX

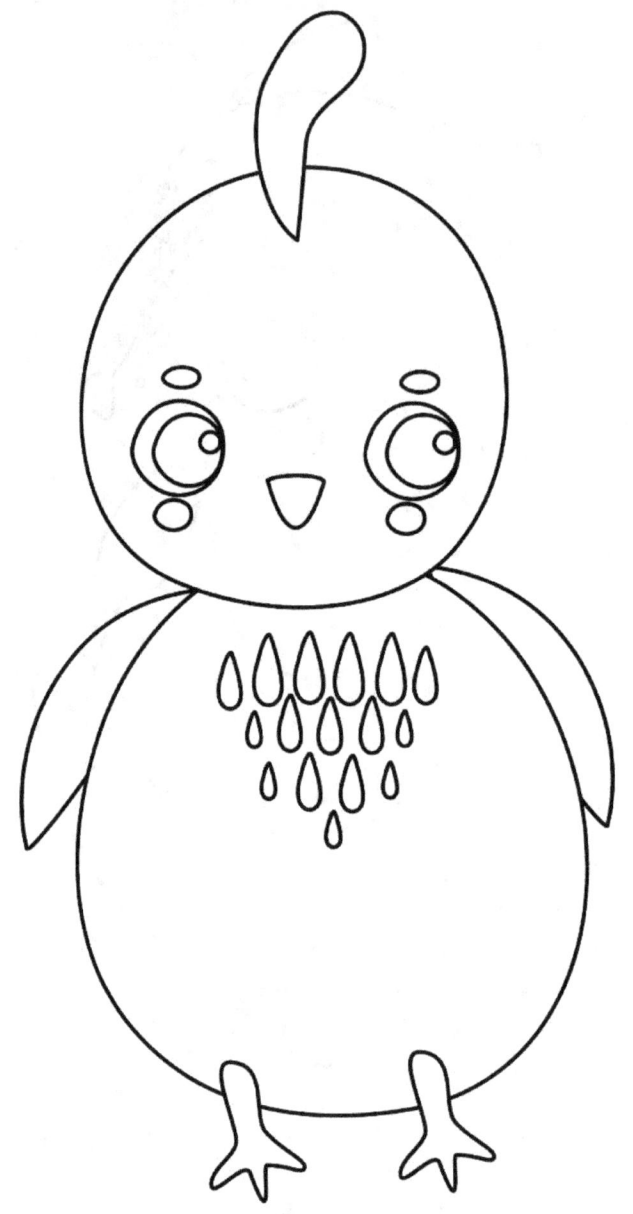

CHICKENS

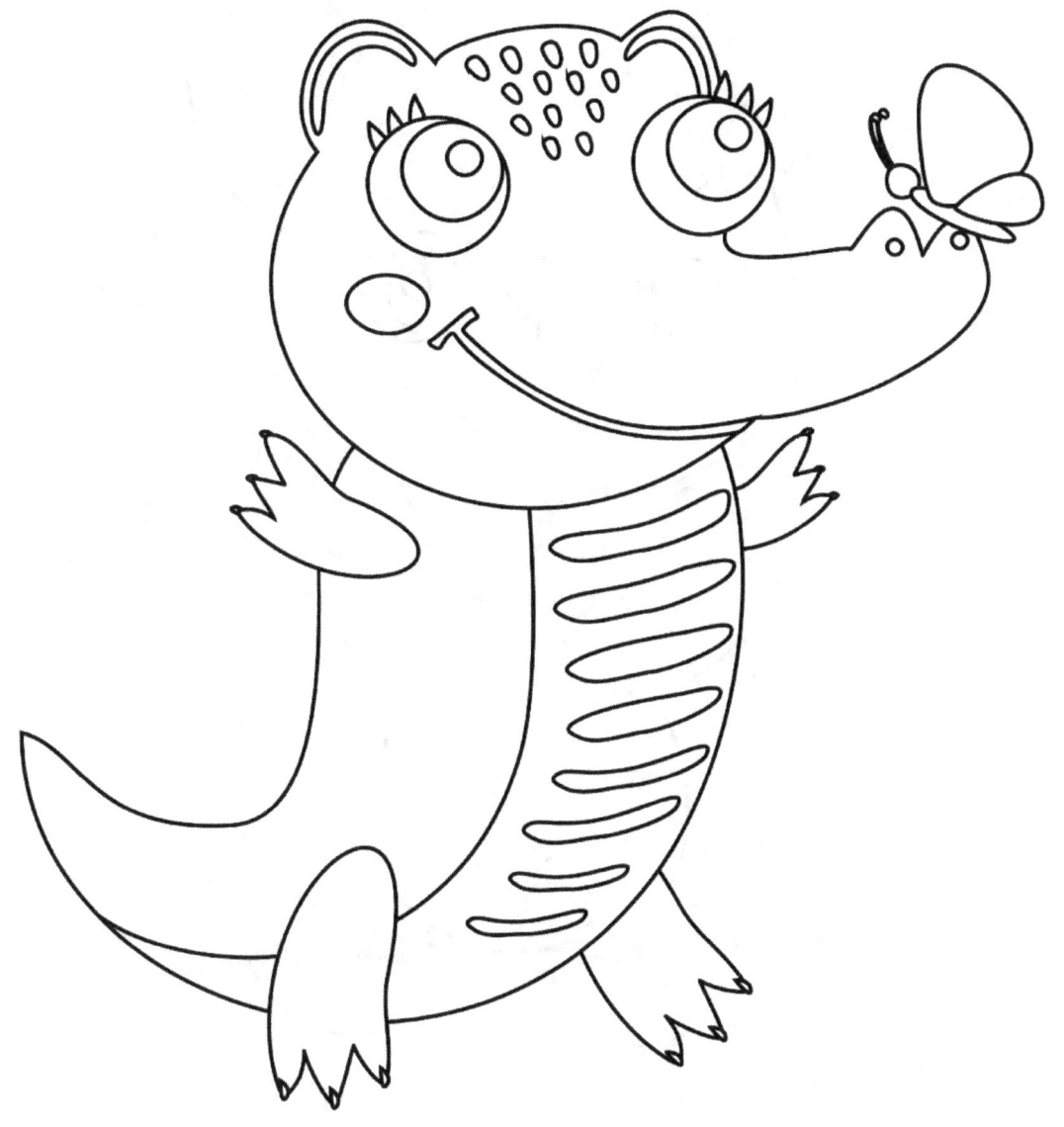

ALLIGATOR

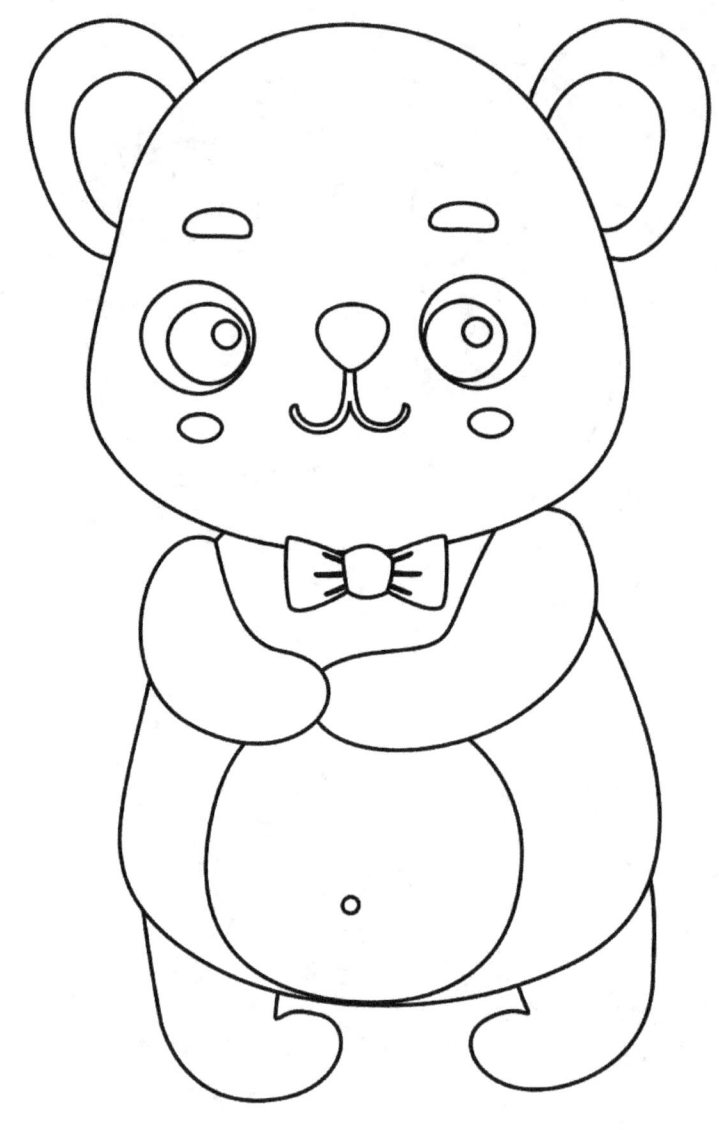

BEAR

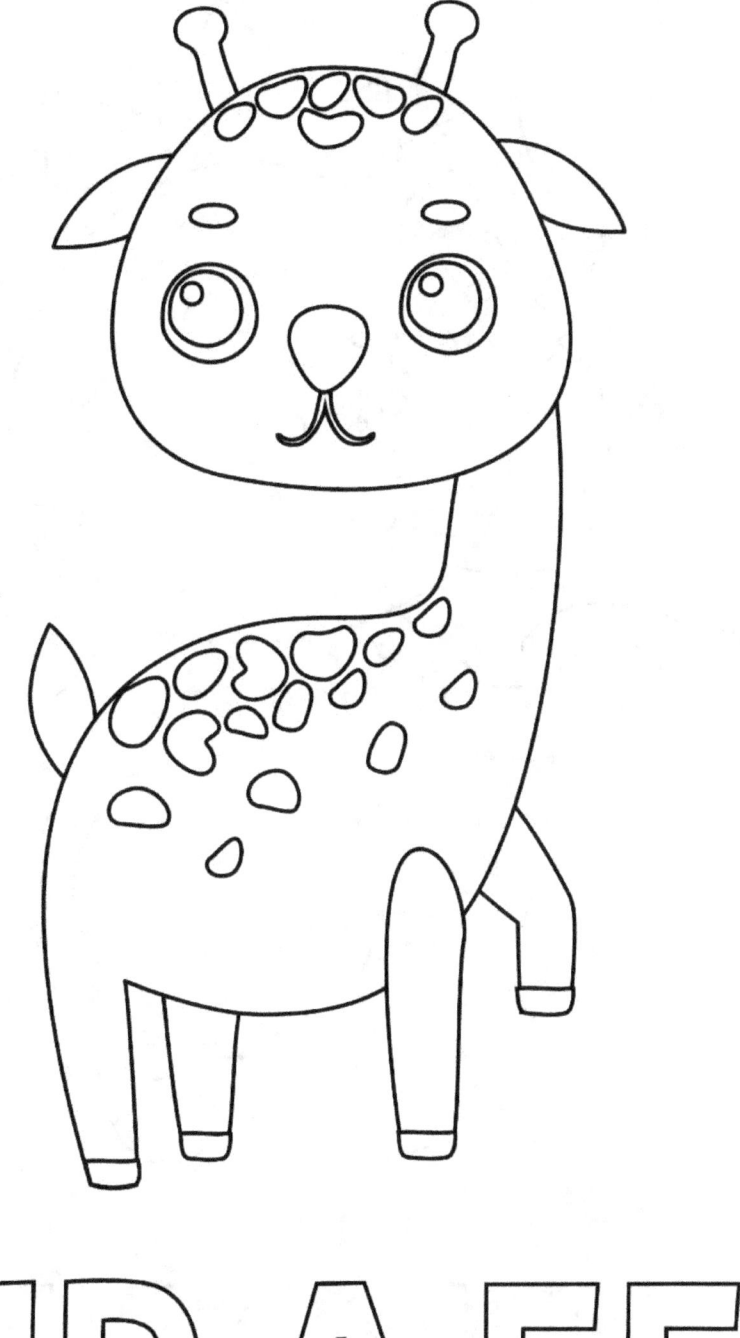

GIRAFFE

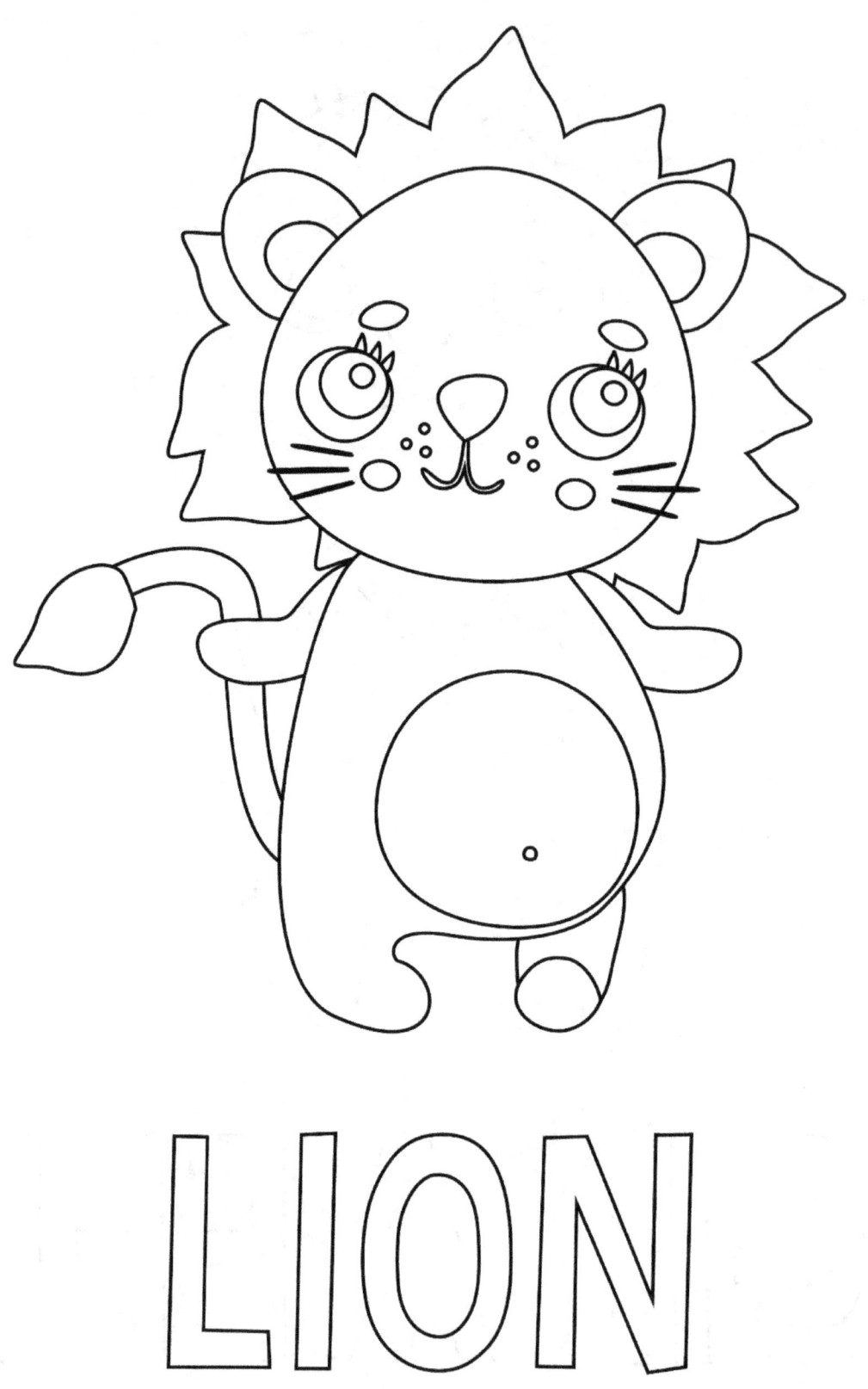

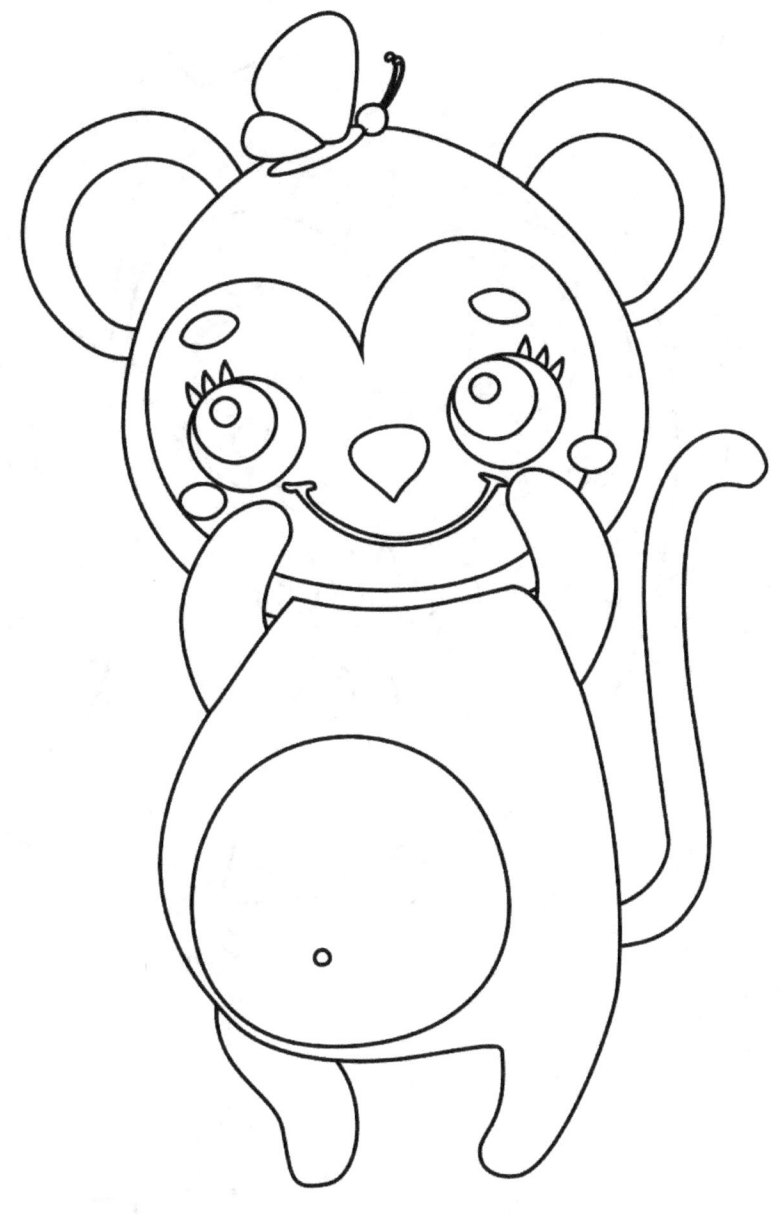

MONKEY

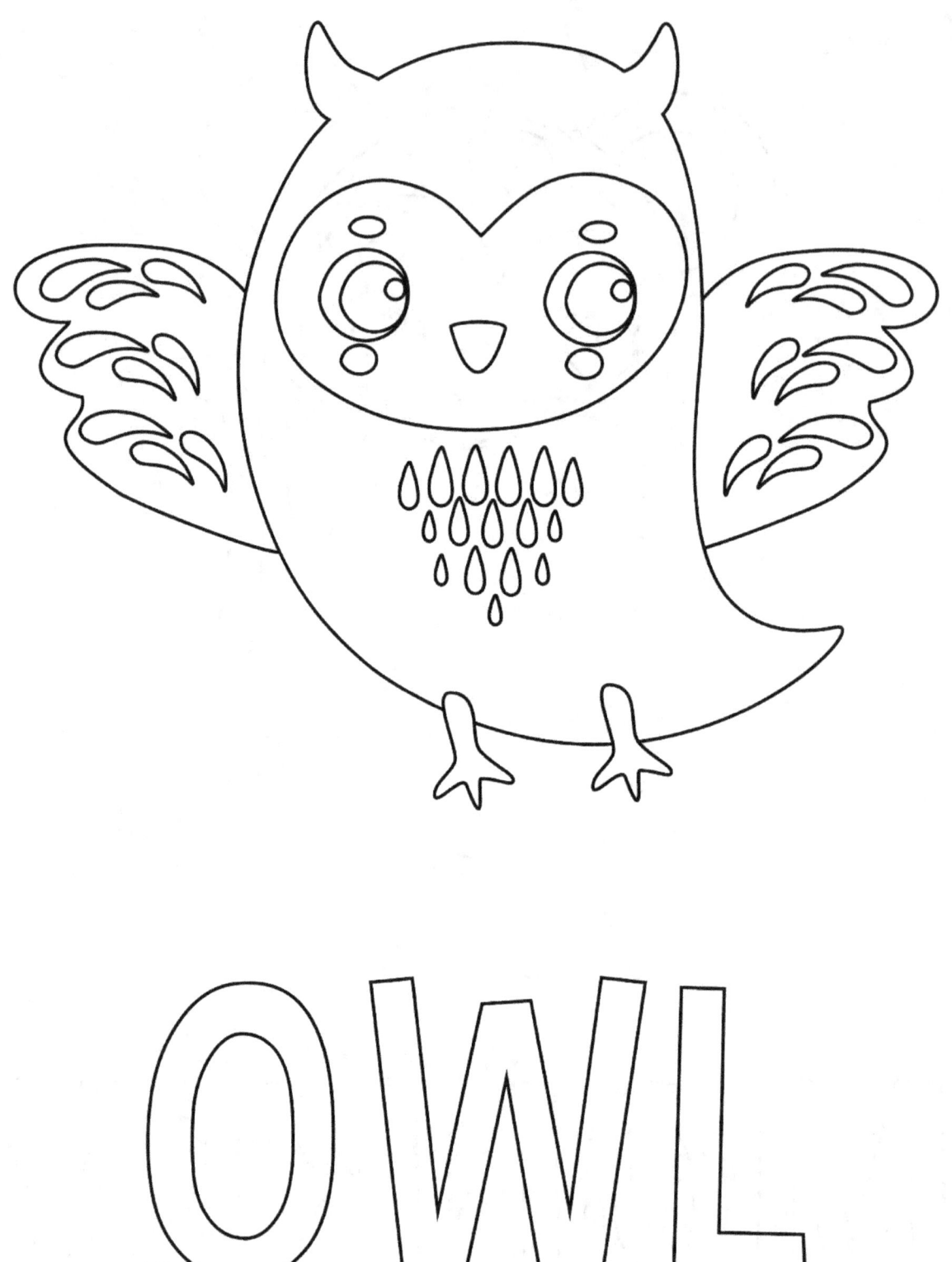

OWL

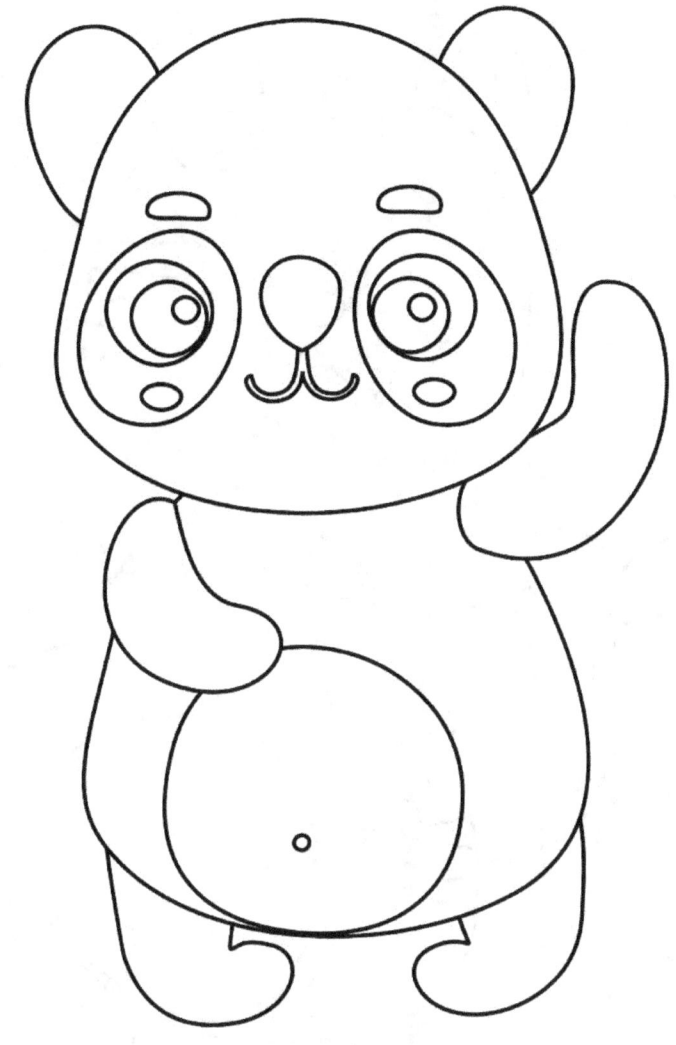

PANDA

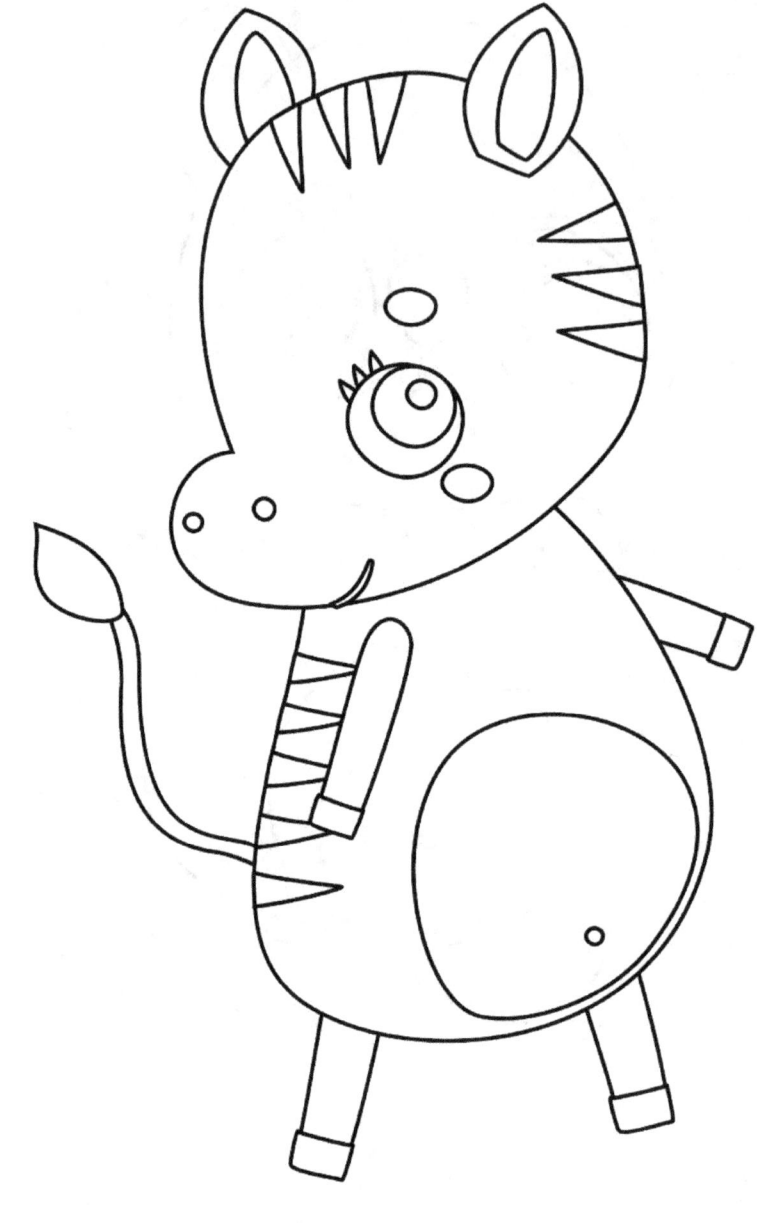

ZEBRA

FOOD

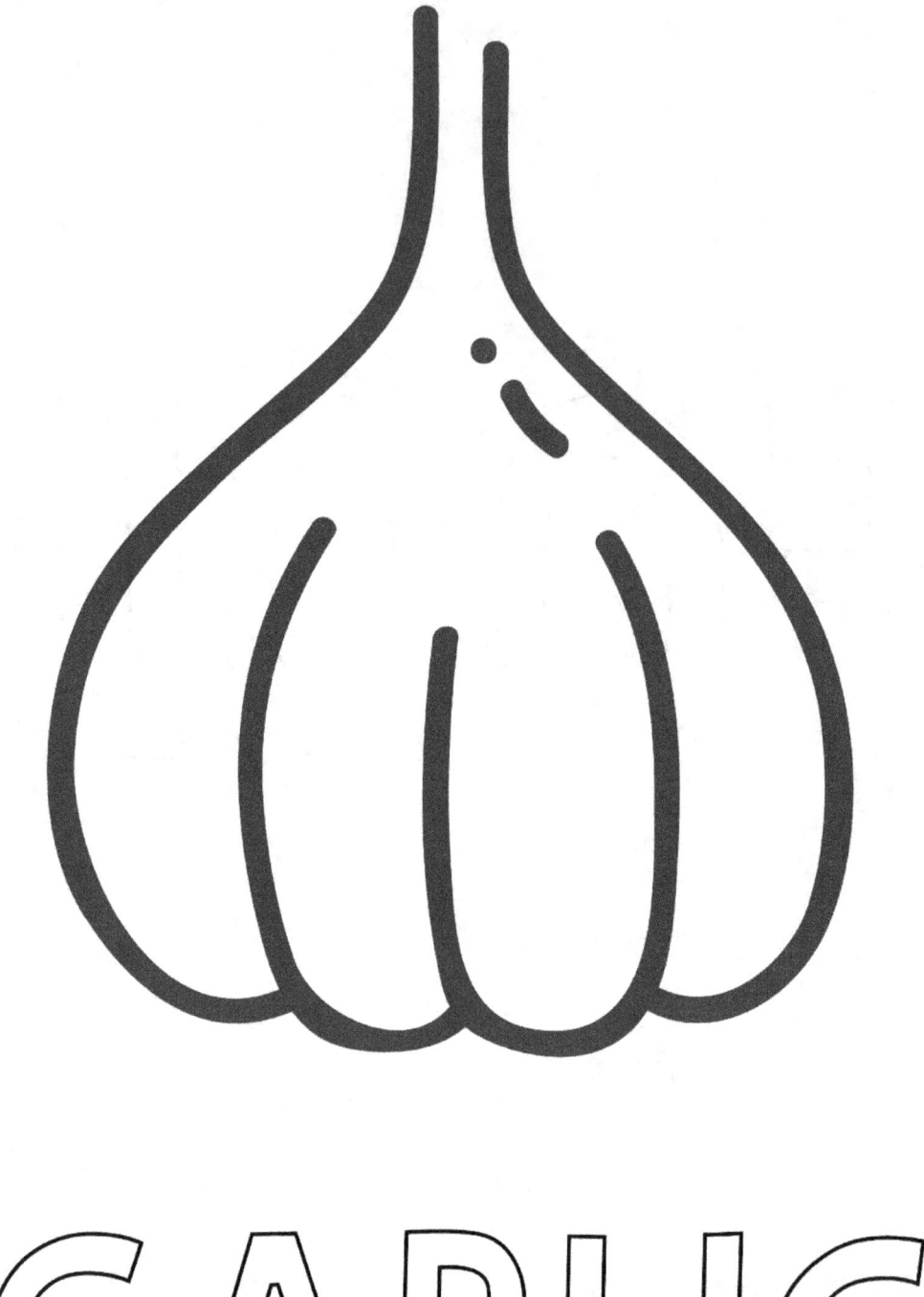

GARLIC

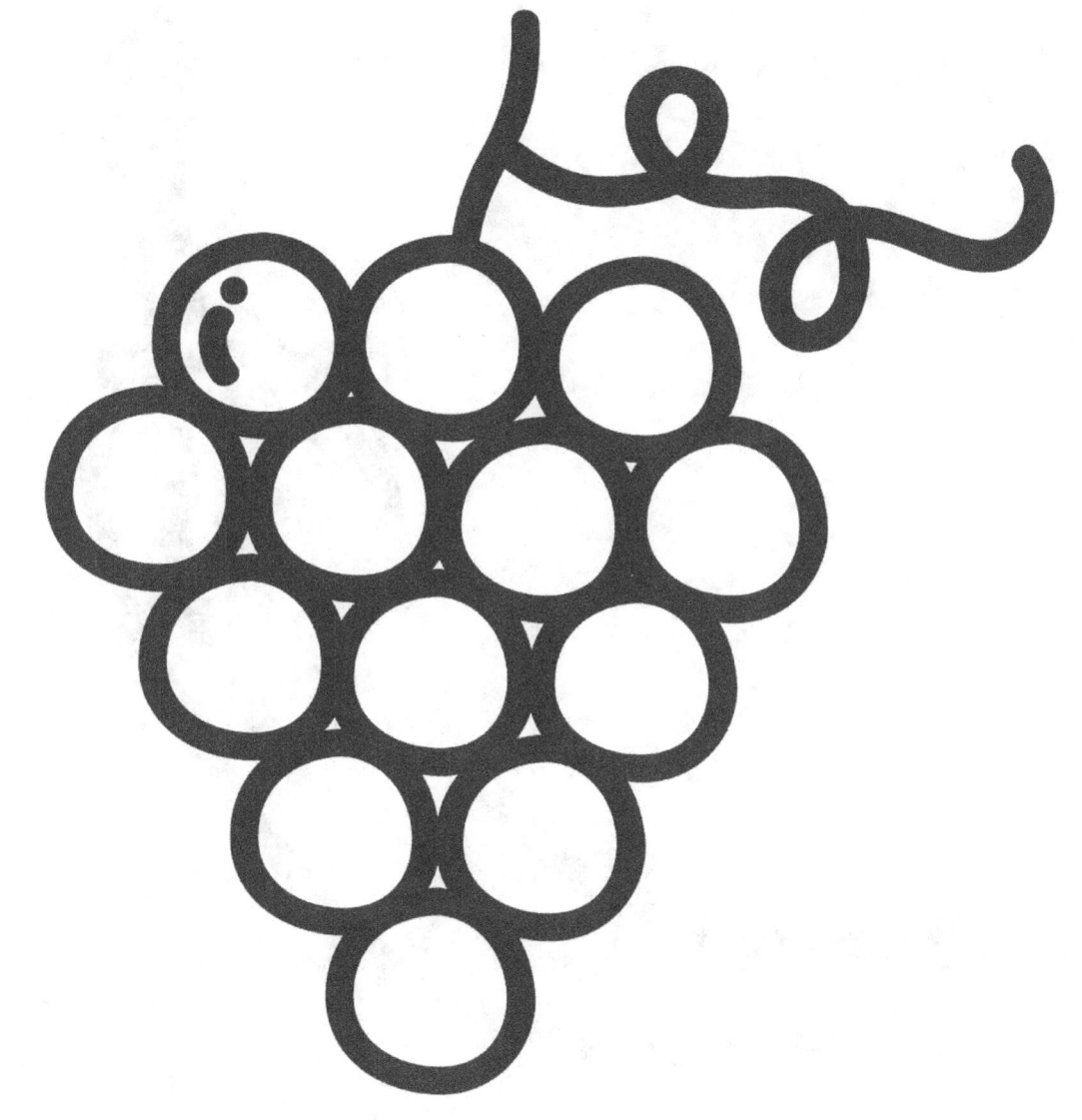

GRAPES

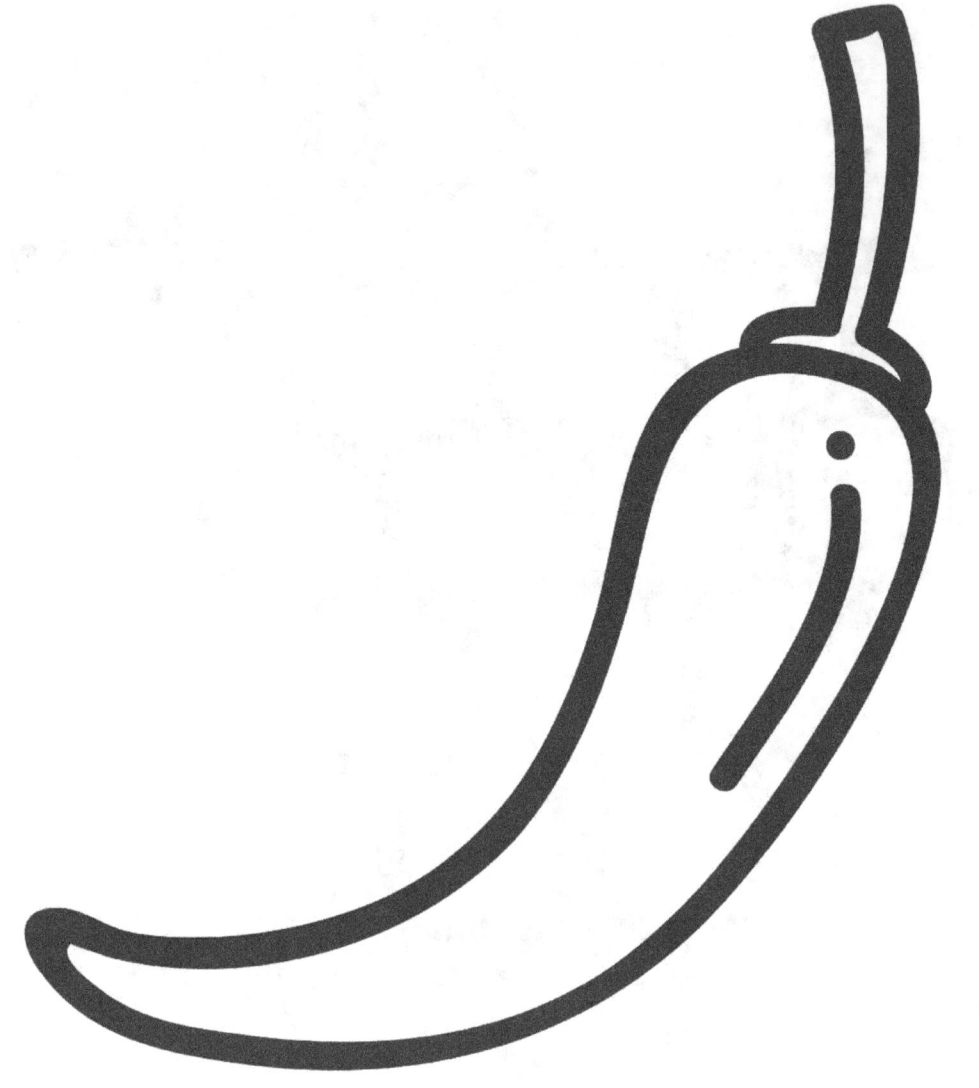

HOT PEPPER

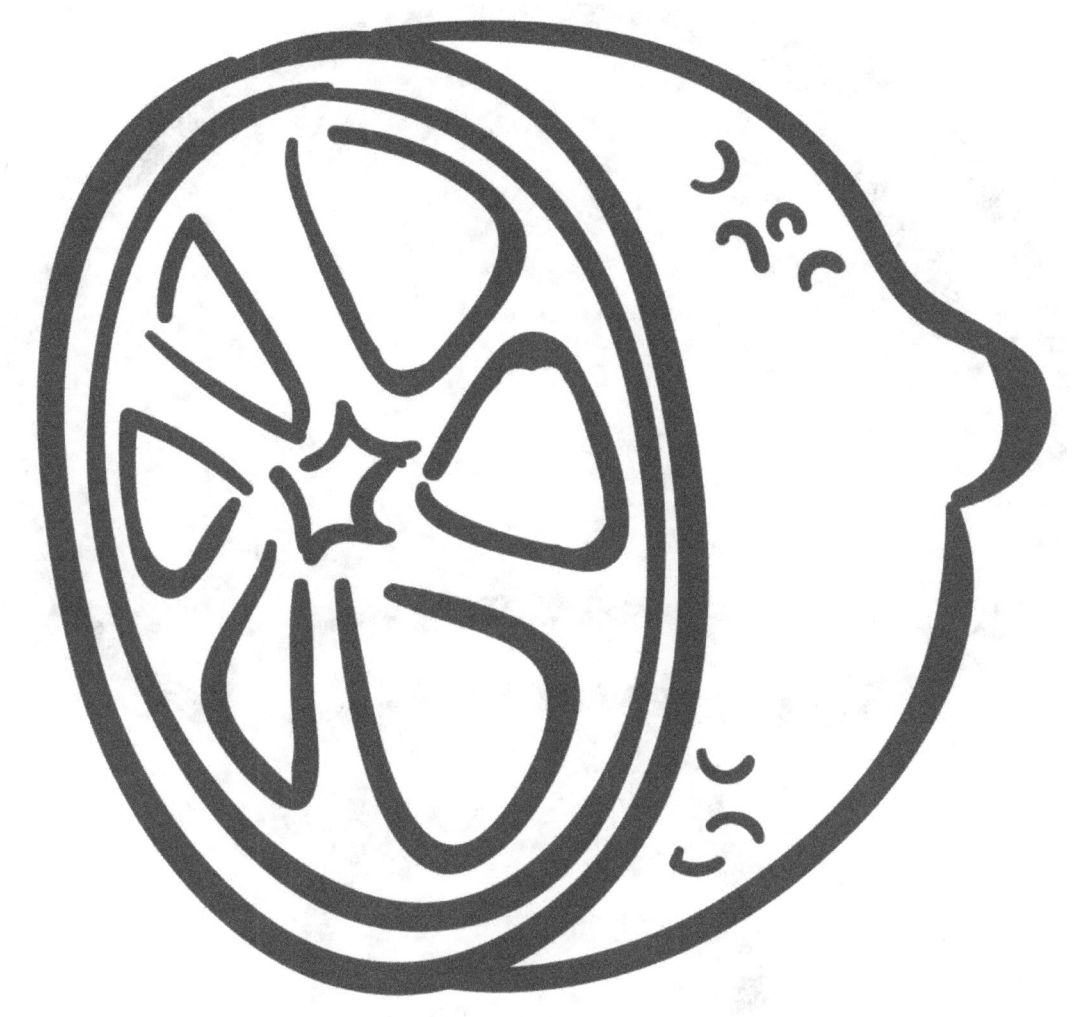

LEMON

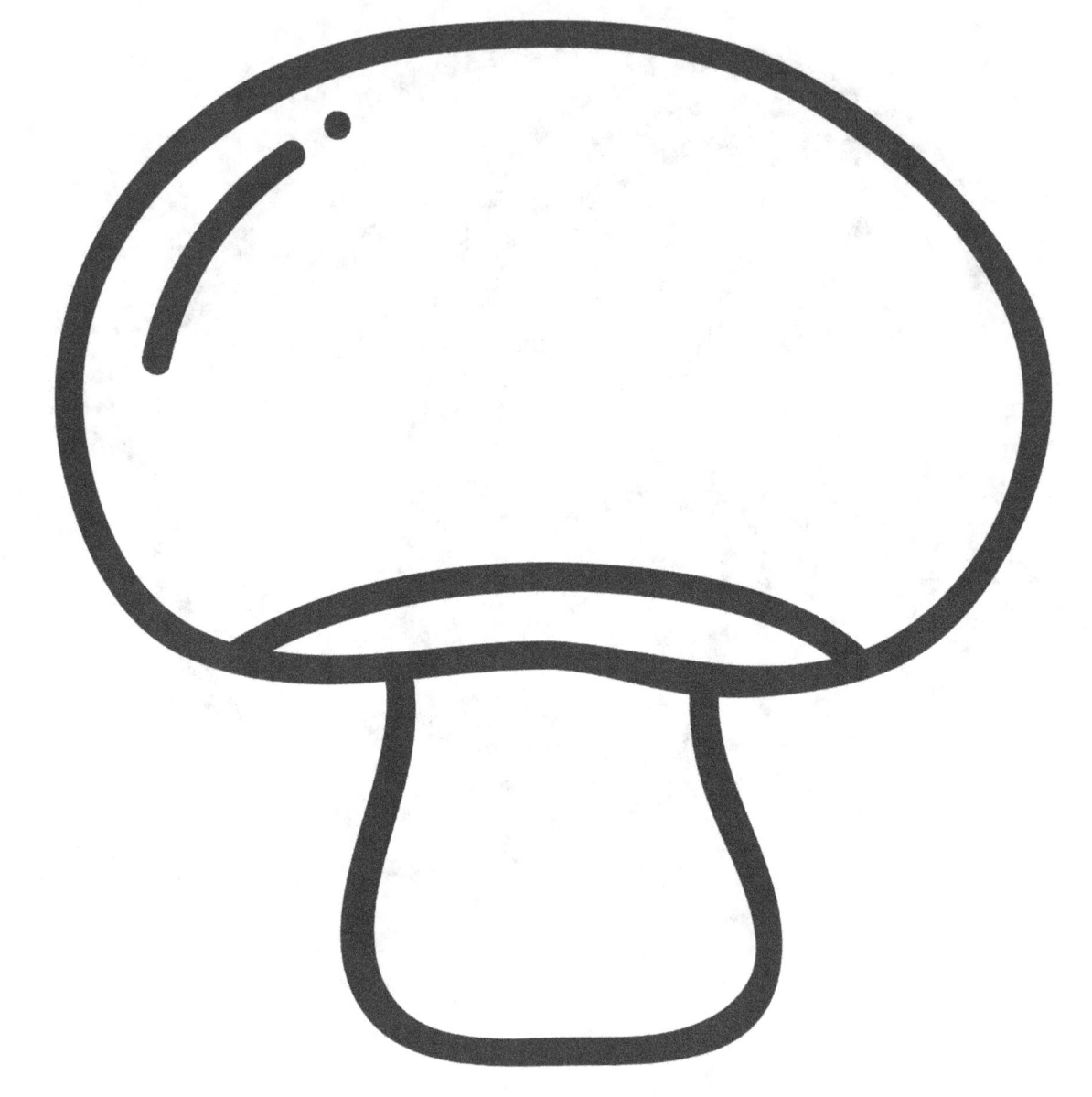

MASHROOMS

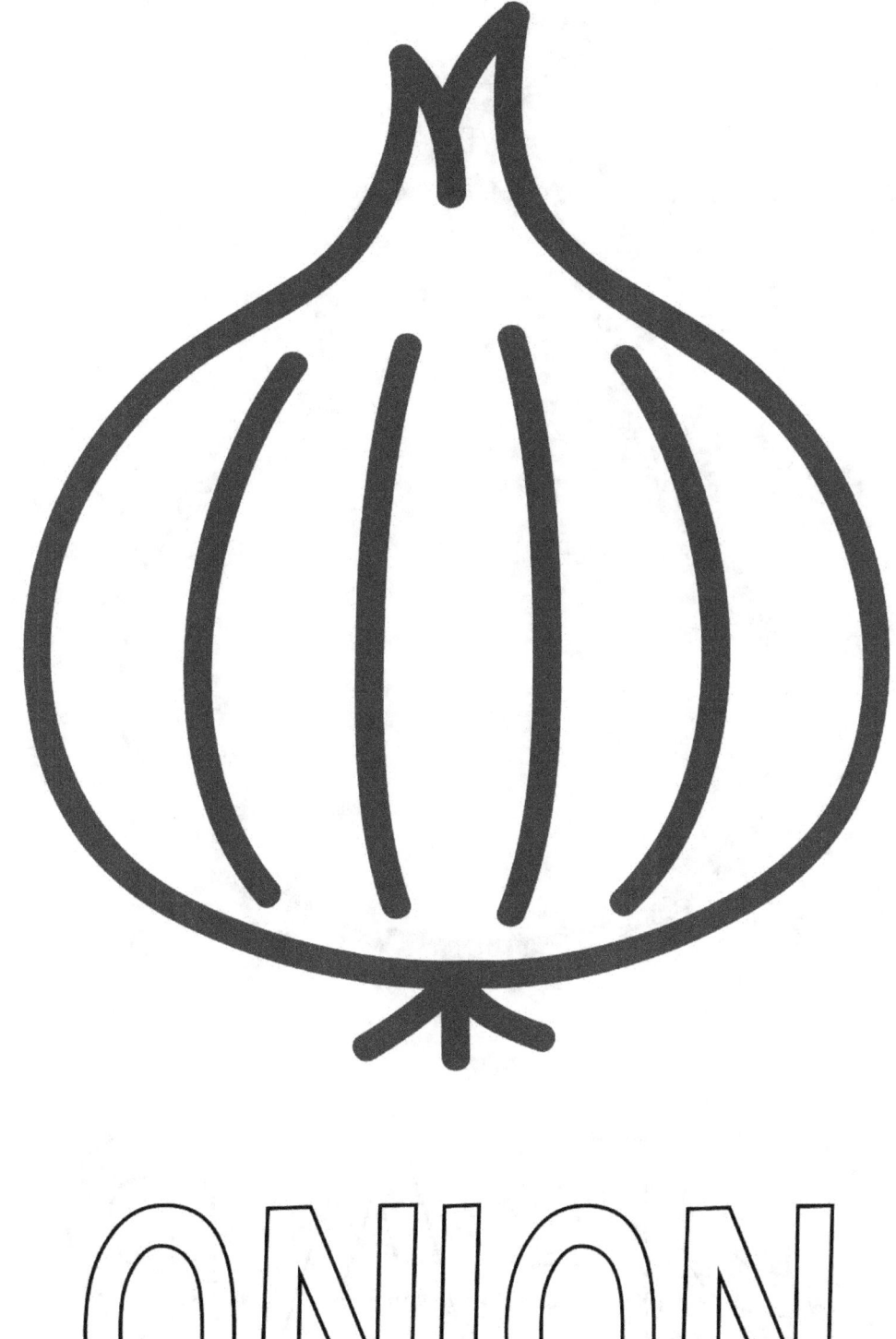

ONION

PEAR

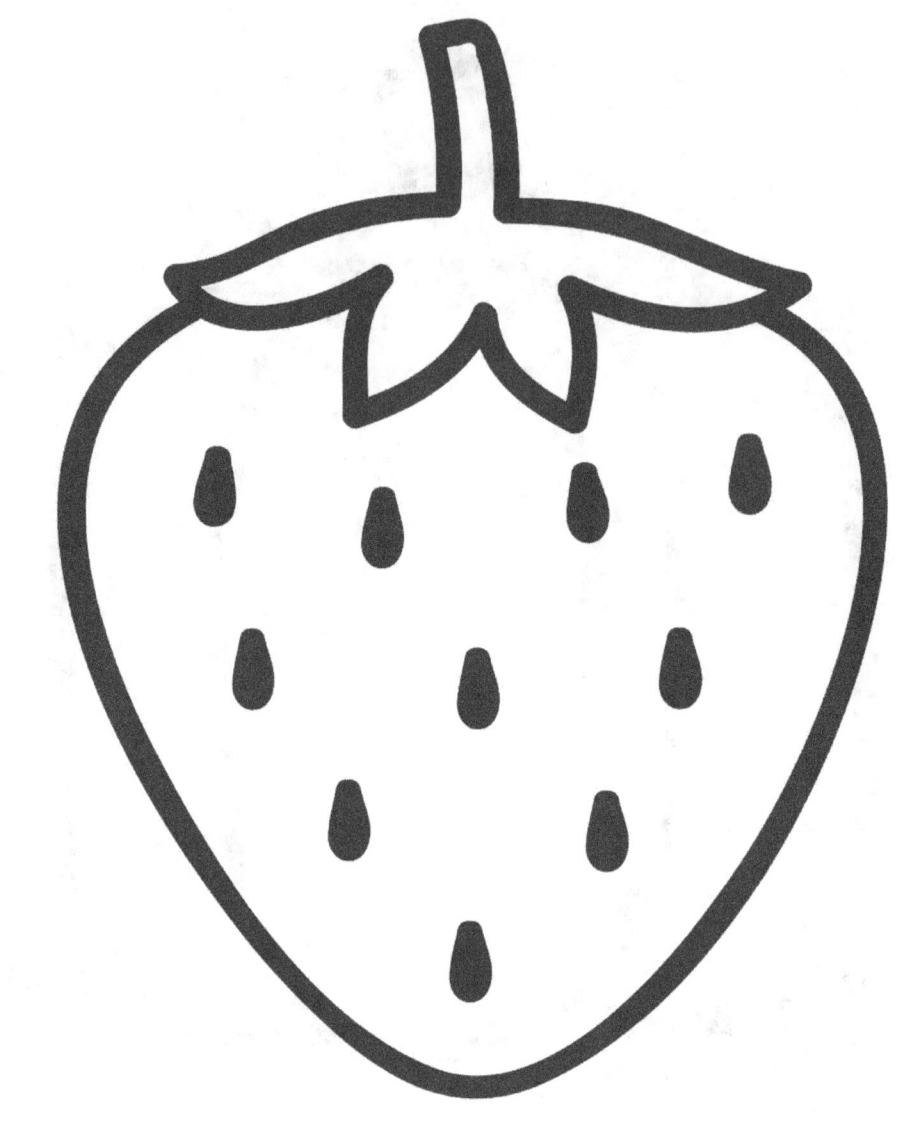

STRAWBERRY

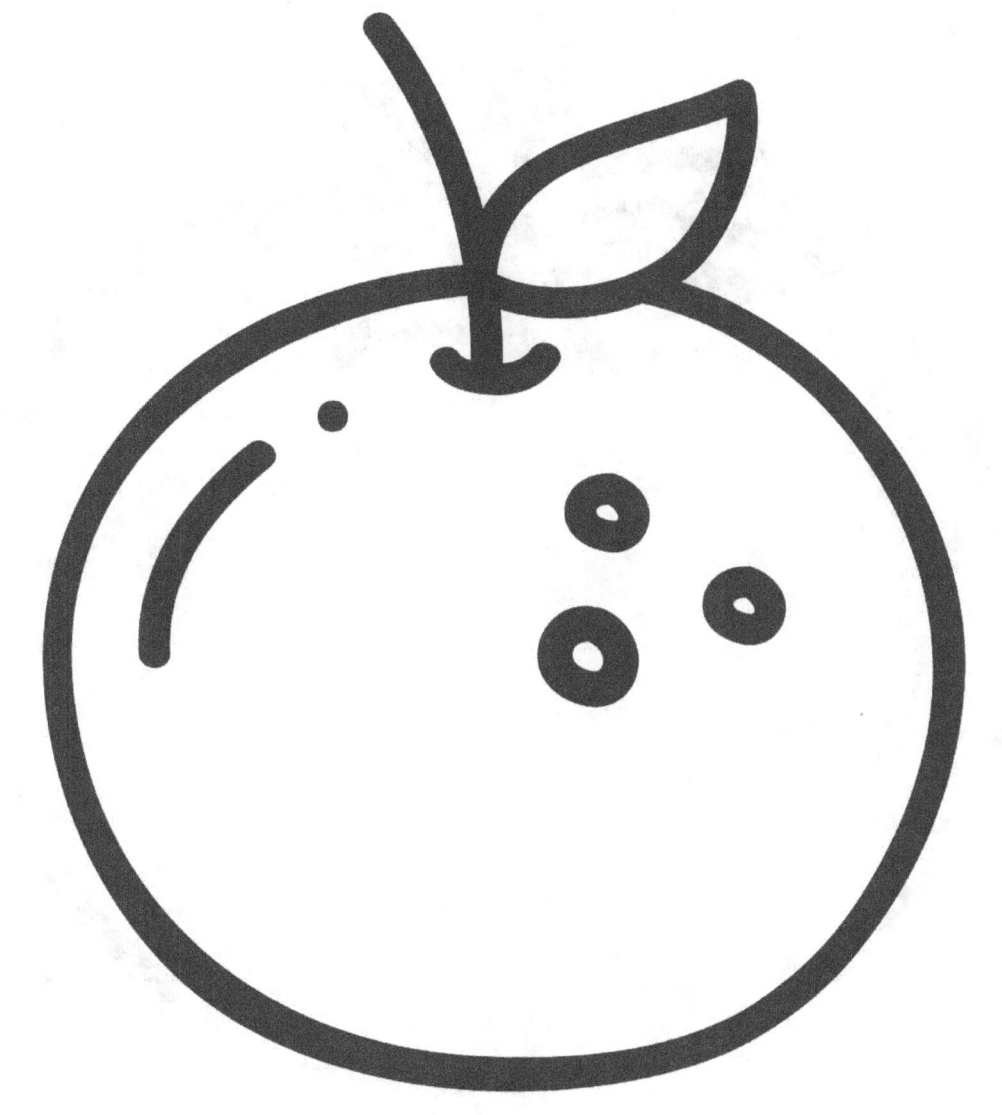

TANGERINE

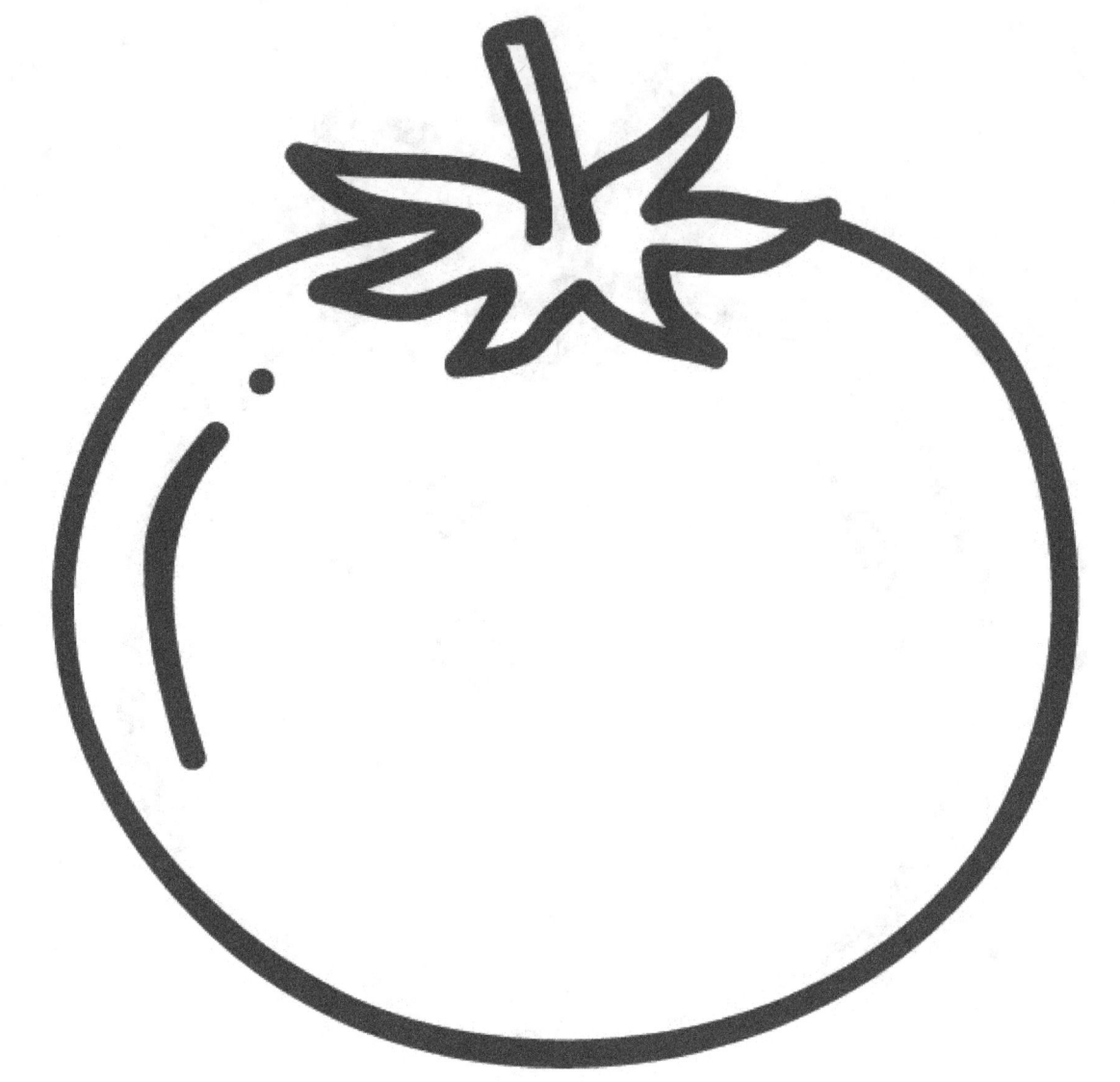

TOMATO

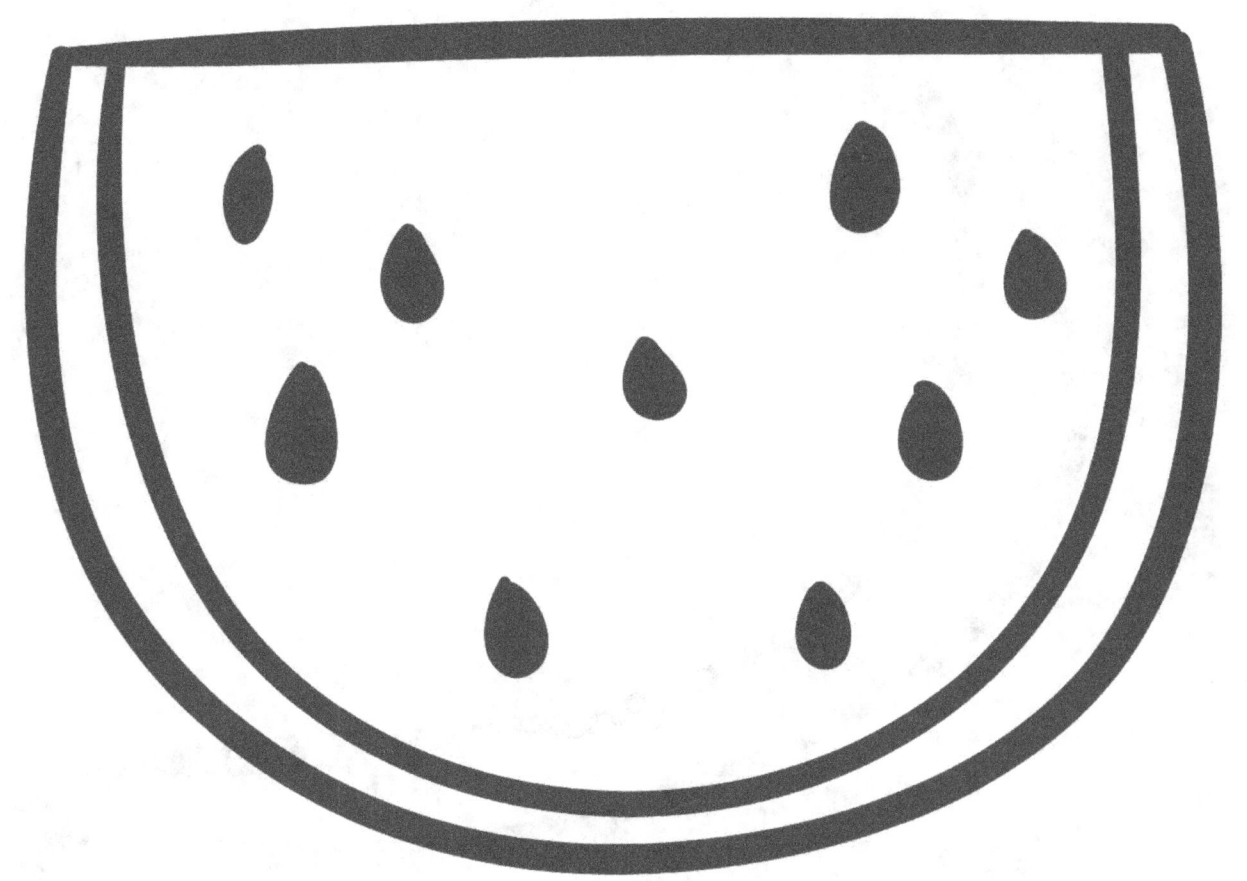

WATERMELON

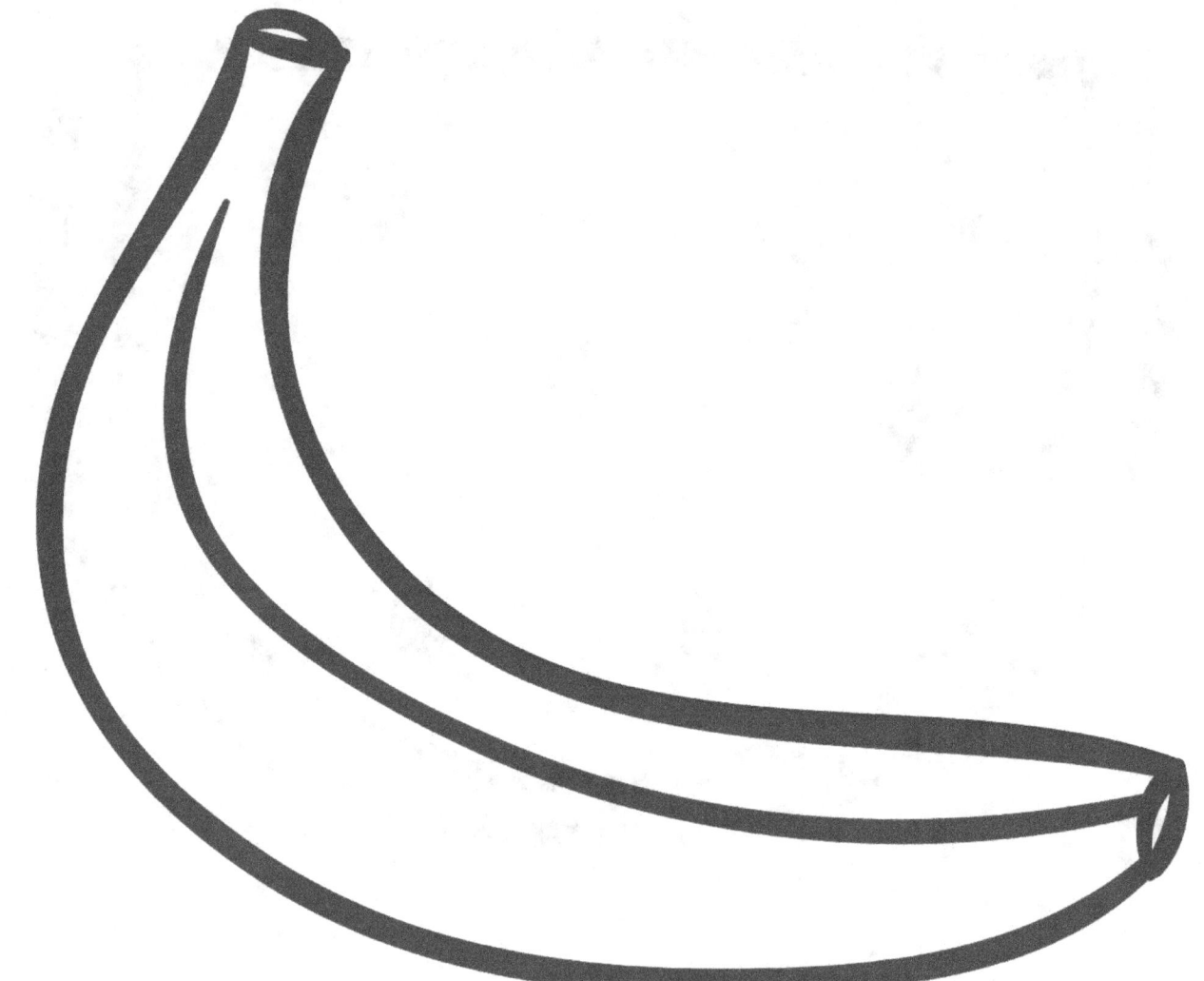

BANANA

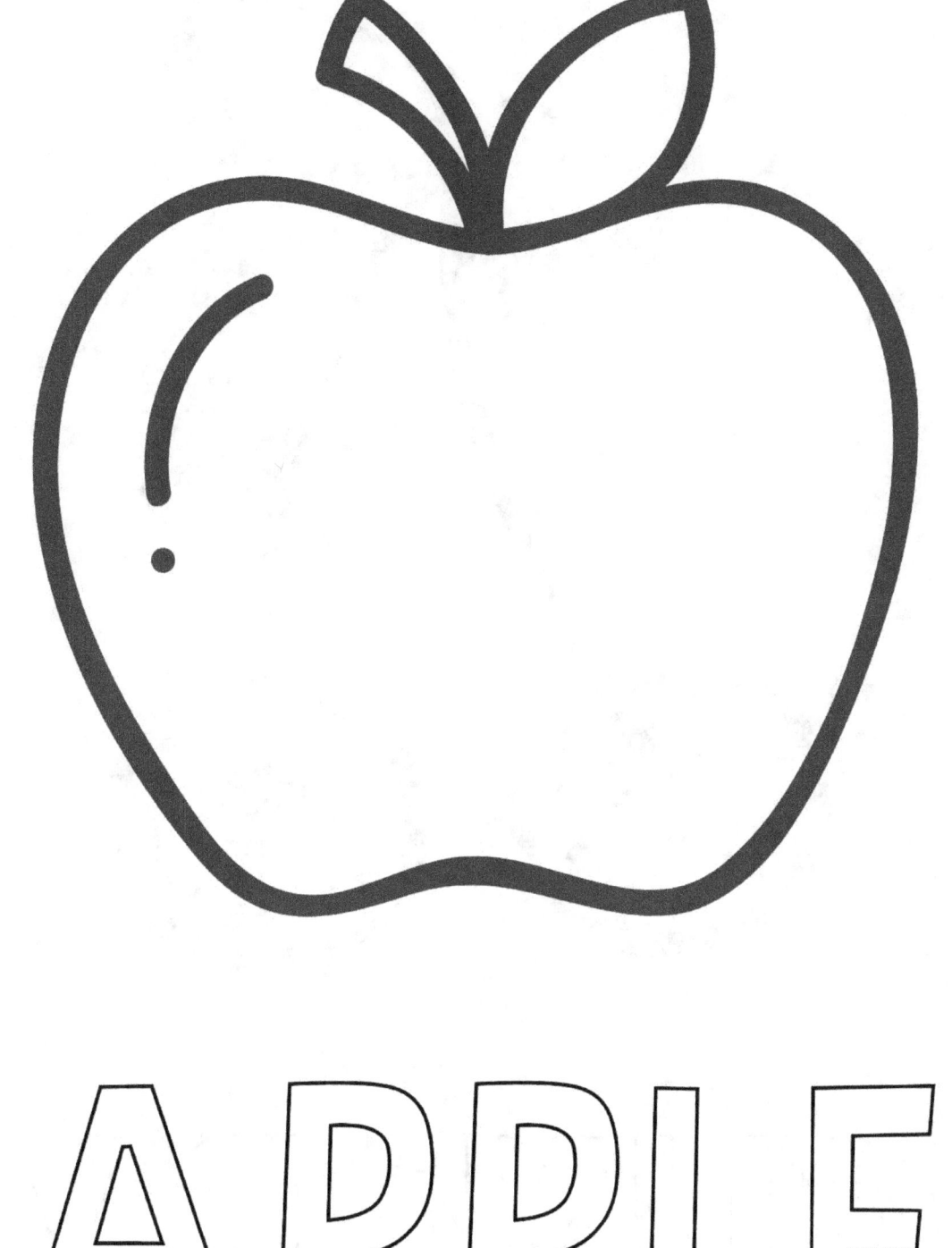

APPLE

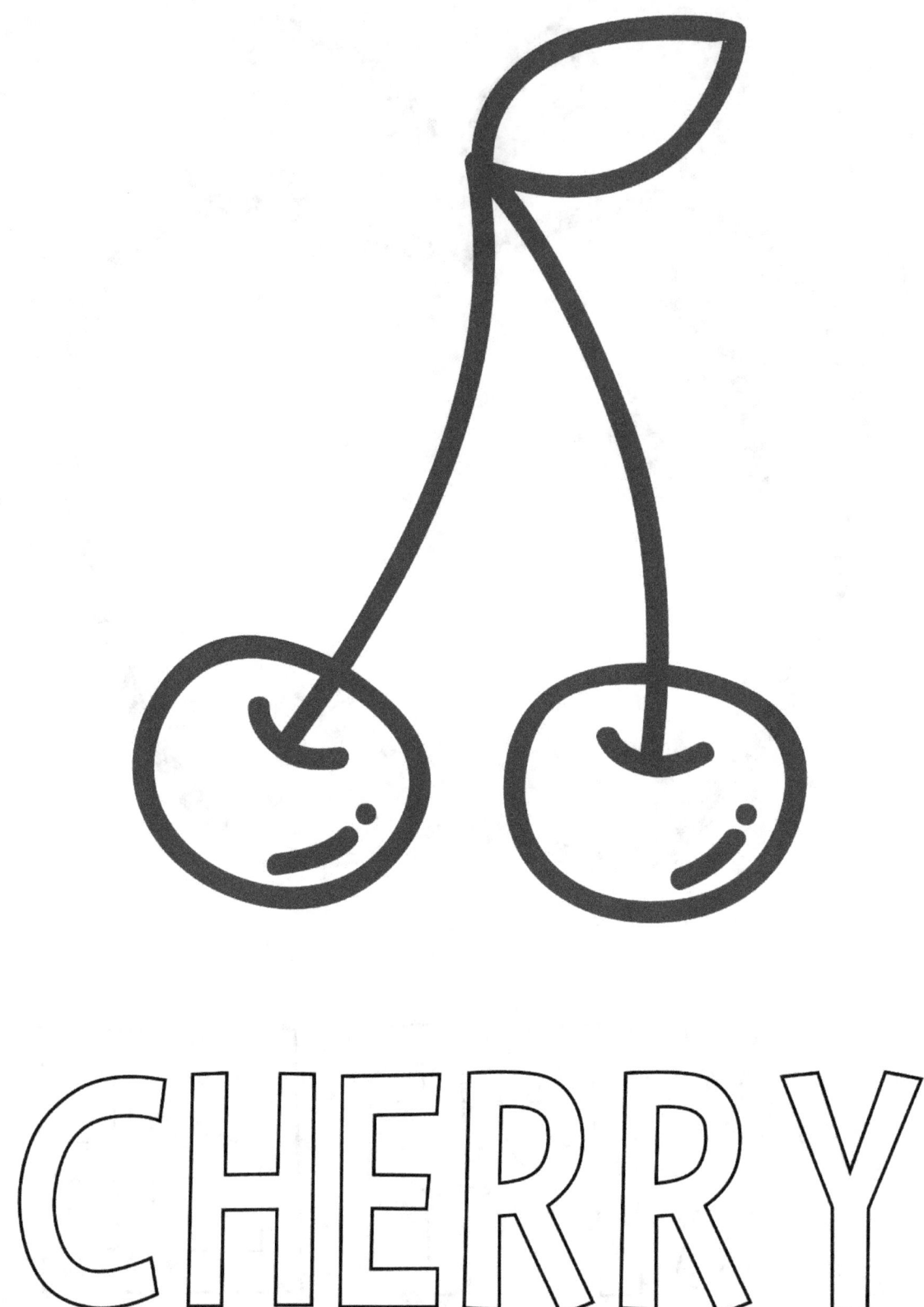

CHERRY

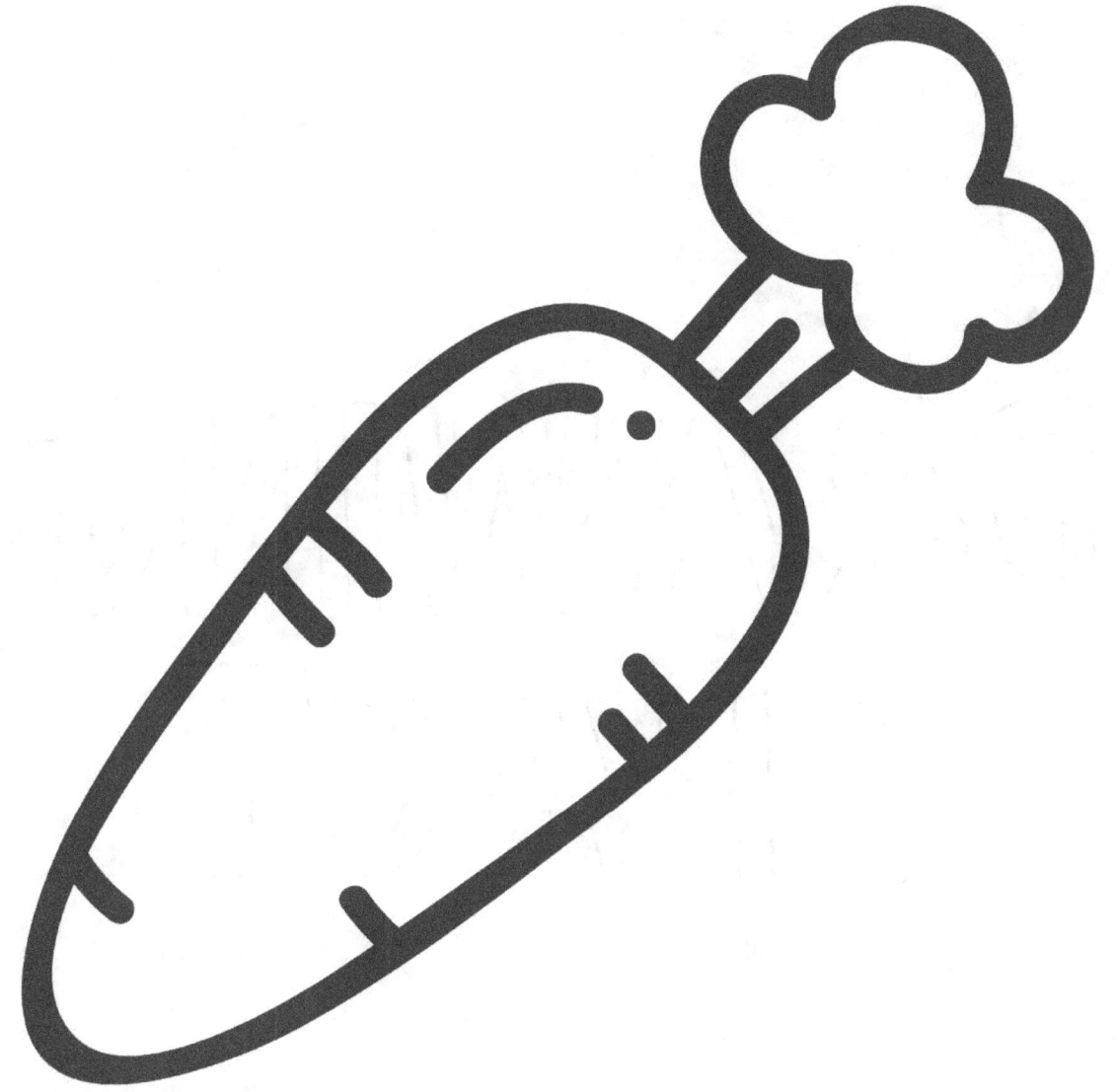

CARROT

DRAWING SPACE

www.ingramcontent.com/pod-product-compliance
Lightning Source LLC
Chambersburg PA
CBHW081449220526
45466CB00008B/2572